MAKERS
OF
MODERN
DALIT
HISTORY

PRAISE FOR THE BOOK

'The book is a ringside view to the early years, breakout period and illustrious contribution of various Dalit personalities in impacting imagination in their chosen fields that has eventually led to the making of Dalit history. It is an attempt to bring back to the mainstream the personalities who tirelessly fought divisive forces and consistently strove to build a socially cohesive society. The book is an important addition to the ever evolving and dynamic Indian literature'—Milind Kamble, founder chairman, Dalit Indian Chamber of Commerce and Industry

'As much as neglect, Dalits have been the objects of condescension and reduced to becoming objects of history. Sudarshan Ramabadran and Guru Prakash Paswan have attempted to rectify this lapse with inspirational stories of Dalits who, apart from overcoming social discrimination, were successful in different fields, from wielding political power to reshaping popular culture. This is a book that will be obligatory reading for all those who seek to understand the totality of the Indian experience'—Swapan Dasgupta, member of Parliament

'Guru Prakash Paswan and Sudarshan Ramabadran are making an important contribution to the emerging canon of Dalit history. The book has a wide sweep. It showcases Dalit poets ranging from Vyasa and Valmiki to Sant Janabhai to Sant Kabir; revolutionaries like Gurram Jashuva and Udham Singh; and leaders from Dakshayani Velayudhan to Ambekdar to Kanshiram. The authors say outright that this is not an endeavour to blame past historians for omission. They want to depart from the prevalent and divisive mood of pessimism that dominates all conversations about social justice by focusing instead on both inspiration and aspiration. The goal is to bring the focus back on the nation as one entity'—Shekhar Gupta, founder and editor-in-chief, ThePrint

'The book is a reminder of the extraordinary Dalit contributions to the history of Indian civilization, from the ancient sages Valmiki and Vyasa to twentieth-century icons Udham Singh and B.R Ambedkar. Young writers Guru and Sudarshan lucidly bring alive half-forgotten characters such as Rani Jhalkaribai, the churn of ideas and the constant pushback against discrimination. Strongly recommended . . .' —Sanjeev Sanyal, writer and economist

MAKERS OF MODERN DALIT HISTORY

SUDARSHAN RAMABADRAN
GURU PRAKASH PASWAN

PENGUIN BOOKS

An imprint of Penguin Random House

PENGUIN BOOKS

USA | Canada | UK | Ireland | Australia
New Zealand | India | South Africa | China

Penguin Books is part of the Penguin Random House group of companies
whose addresses can be found at global.penguinrandomhouse.com

Published by Penguin Random House India Pvt. Ltd
7th Floor, Infinity Tower C, DLF Cyber City,
Gurgaon 122 002, Haryana, India

Penguin
Random House
India

First published in Penguin Books by Penguin Random House India 2021

Copyright © Sudarshan Ramabadran and Guru Prakash Paswan 2021

ISBN 9780143451426

Typeset in Adobe Caslon Pro by Manipal Technologies Limited, Manipal
Printed at Replika Press Pvt. Ltd, India

www.penguin.co.in

MIX
Paper from
responsible sources
FSC® C016779

Contents

Introduction

History provides a reference point for the present and enables us to understand who we are, and therein lies its significance. Quite often, and in general, history has been disregarded as unimportant and irrelevant. This is one of the prima facie reasons that we today do not acutely understand social issues such as caste or conflicts related to caste. We often end up being ignorant of the aberrations that exist in our society and, due to a lack of understanding of history, tend to dismiss them. Thus, to work towards and achieve social integration and cohesion, it becomes imperative that we be not just widely read but also well read about history—especially subaltern history. Only then can we truly assess what has gone wrong over time, and what must now be done to remove the dirt within to reorganize and reinvent as per contemporary times. If not, there is pertinent danger of not equipping young minds with knowledge.

However, being aware and reading history alone may not be enough—preserving or documenting is also the need of the hour. There are social mores that we often acknowledge and honour simply because they have been handed down through the generations. *Makers of Modern Dalit History* is a humble attempt to document some of the creators of Indian history—men and women of the subaltern community who have been forgotten over the years. The book aims to contextualize the lives of these men and women and enable them to be a source of inspiration to the Dalit community and the society at large. Most of the social reformers from the Dalit communities have been redacted from mainstream historical and intellectual discourse. This book is not an attempt to eulogize these individuals but to recognize and acknowledge their contribution to Indian society, and the ill treatment and social ostracization they had to endure to do so.

The Journey

We feel it is essential today to change gears from incredible India to incredible Indians. In this book we have focused on a few such incredible Indians and the life lessons we can draw from them. They not only revolutionized lives but also inspired people and society, catalysing movements by arming themselves with education, knowledge and power.

Of the personalities we have written about in this book, there were those on whom we did find a lot of literature and historical data, but also those on whom we did not find much at all. Therefore, we would like to state that the profiles that the reader will find in this book are a combination of historical facts, stories that people have told about them over generations and popular legends around the lives of those being written about. But the only objective of writing the book is to make sure these personalities don't get lost in the oral retelling of history and that every reader is inspired by the journey these men and women undertook.

When we started listing out the individuals we wanted to cover in this book and approached Meru Gokhale to champion it, in all honesty, we did not have an order in mind. It is just that we felt a wide variety of fields needed to be represented to showcase the tremendous impact they had on society and how they resonated with the people then. We also wanted to choose personalities from diverse regions in and around India. This book largely deals with how they saw spirituality, literature, politics, the freedom movement, economic development and foreign service, to name a few, as instruments of social empowerment.

When we wrote our first column together on Bharat Ratna awardee Bhimrao Ramji Ambedkar for a news daily on 14 April 2016, we were both nervous and anxious, for we knew we had to do justice to the life and work of Babasaheb but also contemporize his words for the readers at large. Although it was a short column, to our surprise, there was organic positive feedback, and we knew then that more such stories of individuals from the socially disadvantaged sections of society had to be brought out as an addendum to the already existing modern Dalit literature we now have. These personalities not only challenged the status quo but also fought against every odd they encountered. We humbly accept that we are no experts, but, as researchers and students of the lives of these personalities, we think the time is ripe for this cause we feel so strongly about to be put into words.

In a lot of ways, this book has been a personal journey for both of us. Since the beginning of our friendship, we have had numerous candid conversations on social hierarchy and untouchability in cabs, at dining tables, at metro stations, at airports, at railway stations, during visits to villages, at conferences and seminars, over WhatsApp exchanges, calls and texts. These conversations have not just helped us understand each other better and forge an unbreakable bond of friendship, but also encouraged us to stand up for the cause of social cohesion and do our bit. Even if it was a subtle social media meme jocularly siding with casteism, it hurt us no end. All this only provoked us to think and contribute constructively in our own way. It is in this process that, apart from writing, we started doing our bit by organizing unique intellectual initiatives across the country—in Chennai, Mumbai, Delhi and Patna. Our intention was to bring together multiple stakeholders to reimagine our society, revolutionize our thinking and philosophy on caste, and come together as a united and cohesive society. To our delight, we noticed the openness with which these cities were willing to participate in a dialogue to abolish discrimination. We understand there is yet a long road to travel. But travel we must.

Modern Dalit Literature

The history of modern Dalit literature has its origins in Maharashtra. It is here that the first Dalit writers' conference was held, which eventually led to the Dalit Panthers movement. Eleanor Zelliot, an American scholar of Ambedkar, who has also written on the emergence of Dalit movements and Dalit literature, writes,

> In the early 1970s two Maharashtrian movements achieved enough prominence to be noticed by the English press, the Dalit panthers and Dalit literature. By substituting the word 'Black' for 'Dalit' the reader can immediately understand that a phenomenon comparable to the American Black Panthers and Black literature has surfaced among the lower caste in social and literary affairs in Western India. Like the American movements, the Dalit panthers and the Dalit School of literature represent a new level of pride, militancy and sophisticated creativity.[1]

Subaltern literature in India has evolved into a strong medium for the community to express its angst, emotions and experiences in words. In his time, which is the nineteenth century, Mahatma Jyotirao Phule, a subaltern icon, was the architect of subaltern literature. Such literature, of and by those from the subaltern community, instilled in the minds of the readers a spirit of inquiry and made them understand that education was the only means by which empowerment and progress could be achieved. Phule's *Gulamgiri* (meaning slavery), published in 1885, was a scathing attack against the caste system, calling for the emancipation of the Dalits.

Among the foremost catalysts of ancient Indian literature spearheaded by Dalits were Sage Vyasa and Sage Valmiki. Indian literature is incomplete without highlighting the contribution of these two men. As Babasaheb Ambedkar himself said, 'The Hindus wanted the Vedas, they sent for Vyasa, who was not a caste Hindu. The Hindus wanted an epic, they sent for Valmiki, who was an untouchable. The Hindus wanted a Constitution, and they have sent for me.'[2]

Subaltern literature has today come to represent the quest for dignity. It has truly signified a rebellion with three principle pillars—liberty, equality and fraternity. It is a testament to the sheer will and resilience of the community, who have been for long denied their right to articulate their thoughts. Dalits have also begun to use their surnames in various literary forms that they bring out to highlight their plight. For example, the Bengali Dalit writer Manoranjan Byapari has published his autobiography titled *Interrogating My Chandal Life: An Autobiography of a Dalit*,[3] and another Bengali poet and activist, Kalyani Thakur, added 'Charal' to her surname, indicating that she was proud of being a Chandal, one of the untouchable communities.[4]

There has been Dalit literature that has garnered recent interest and been republished to illustrate the treatment of the community.

One striking example is the hard-hitting essay by Muktabai, who, as a girl, studied in one of the schools set up by the Phules in Pune. The eleven-year-old wrote on what it meant to be a Mang or a Mahar. She went on to highlight how her community was exploited and dispossessed of land. This essay was published in 1855, by *Dnayodaya*, an Ahmednagar-based journal.[5]

Another example of Dalit literature prior to political independence in 1947 is a poem by Hira Dom from the Central Provinces, titled *Acchut ki Shikayat* (An Untouchable's Complaint). This was published in the September 1914 issue of the Hindi magazine *Saraswati*. In the subsequent year, Mohini Chamarin, a Dalit woman from the same province as Dom, published a short story, *Chhot ke Shor* (Thieves of the Subordinated), in the August 1915 issue of a Hindi magazine named *Kanya Manorajan*. However, as mentioned earlier, recent interest in these writings has encouraged further curiosity in understanding the literature produced then.[6] Some scholars say that Arjun Dangle's *Poisoned Bread: Translations from Modern Marathi Dalit Literature*[7] is believed to have been the first edited anthology of Dalit writing in English.

In all this, the contribution of the Maharashtra Dalit Sahitya Sangh cannot be undermined, as it was greatly responsible for the resurgence in Dalit literature. The first conference of Dalit writers was organized in Bombay (now Mumbai) in 1958. Later, this led to the founding of the Dalit Panthers movement. Almost all of those in the movement were writers. Resolution 5 of the conference stated that 'the literature written by the Dalits and that written by others about Dalits in Marathi be accepted as a separate entity known as Dalit literature, and realizing its cultural importance, the universities and literary organisations should give it its proper place'.[8]

Dalit literature is not only about hunger, poverty, oppression and subjugation; it is also about the resistance of the disempowered against the negative forces put in place by dominant groups.

On the other hand, Dalit feminist writers have recovered their own history of the Dalit movement. According to a 2008 book, *We Also Made History*, which was largely based on the interviews of women, Dalit women's unique role was documented as participating and strengthening the Ambedkarite movement in the 1940s and providing it with an unusual social depth in the Vidarbha region of western India.[9]

Another fascinating aspect of Dalit literature has been the achievements of Punjabi Dalit literature, especially its intellectual poets. No other language perhaps has so far had Dalit literature of such high literary calibre. The poets envision an egalitarian and just social order. Forged from the direct experiences of untouchability, they forcefully attack caste divisions, using the stock of available ideas—ancient Advaita Vedanta, Nathism, Sufism or Sikhism—to argue that all such divisions are unnatural and man-made.[10]

Dalit literature in the 1990s has also been an important addendum. One important work is Narendra Jadhav's *Outcaste: A Memoir*, which represents Dalit life in a global space whose boundaries extend beyond the nation. The book has attracted wide critical acclaim all over the world. The book was written by Jadhav when he was in Washington D.C. for over four years. The important shift that Jadhav made in this book was from the Indian national context and its constitutional framework to the global context.[11]

In keeping with the changing contours of modern Dalit literature, the attempt through *Makers of Modern Dalit History* is to facilitate the stream of Dalit studies. The emergence of Dalit studies as a discipline has also had a notable trajectory. In 1991–92, when V.P. Singh celebrated Ambedkar's birth centenary, Ambedkar chairs were established in universities to facilitate research on Dalit issues and literature. It is against this background that Arjun Dangle's edited anthology, *Poisoned Bread: Translations from Modern Marathi Dalit Literature*, the first English translation of modern Marathi Dalit writings, came out in 1992. Enthusiasm grew and so did the emergence of the discipline called Dalit studies in the 1990s.[12] Like gender studies or cultural studies, Dalit studies have been established as a course in various colleges and universities. Unfortunately, the number of institutions offering Dalit studies or courses on Dalit issues in India is very few.[13]

Today, modern Dalit literature is over five decades old, but to understand the real issues concerning the community, we need to understand not just theories but its history—for the achievements are worthy and commendable. It is in this context that recorded history—not just popular culture, which is often based on hearsay or word of mouth—is essential. There have been significant aspects of subaltern movements that have been ignored by writers for reasons best known to them.

One glaring example is that of the Pasi community. R.K. Chaudhary, who hails from the Pasi community of Uttar Pradesh, has rued the fact that not much has been written or spoken about it. In his words:

> The moot point is this—scholars have never identified communities such as the Pasi as a subject of study, even though Udadevi and Makka Pasi are the only Dalit couple to have been martyred, during the 1857 war of independence.[14]

Twenty-first-century historians in India must examine why these important aspects in Dalit history have not been given enough attention. Dalit literature must, in our view, factor in new paradigms of social justice while affirming the new Dalit identity that can inspire today's generation. The focus has to be on inspiration as well as aspiration, and that is what we have strived to do in this book.

Blaming the architects and writers of history is not our intention. Indian history is replete with contributions of men and women who have sacrificed everything for the sake of our culture and nation. We want to remember and pay homage to those who contributed from the margins as well.

As Yuval Noah Harari, the famous Israeli author, has written, 'History and lessons from the past are essential because by reading about it, one tends to be liberated from it.'[15] In presenting these personalities to the reader, we aim to enable the reader to be aware of some of the most unexpected and unthinkable atrocities heaped on these people in their quest to establish equality, integration and cohesion in society.

We hope that by exploring their lives, each one of us can take strong and certain strides in learning and being 'liberated' from some of the critical aberrations made in the past, so we may be able to carve out an India that seeks divinity and happiness as a cohesive society.

The Importance of the Term 'Dalit'

The term 'Dalit' has had a chequered past. Prior to the adoption of the term as an identity, its people were addressed by different names such as Chandalas, Hinajatians, Avarnas, Antyajas, Acchuts, Pariahs, Namasudras, Untouchables, Unapproachables, Outcastes and Panchamas. It must be noted that the term 'depressed classes' was used for these castes predominantly by social reformers. However, the root of this term's first usage and context is unknown. Ambedkar, too, used this term often in his writings and discourses, in addition to using the word 'untouchables'. Some other terms that also began to gain traction were 'suppressed classes' and 'oppressed Hindus'. Another important term by which the Dalits began to be identified was 'Harijan'. This was first used by Narsinh Mehta, a Gujarati poet-saint of the Bhakti tradition.

It is in Marathi that the frequent use of the term 'Dalit' is also recorded. The Marathi version of the term 'Dalit' was first used in the 1831 edition of *Molesworth's Marathi–English Dictionary*, which was later reprinted in 1975.[16] The founding of the Dalit Panthers movement in Maharashtra in 1972 by J.V. Pawar, Namdeo Dhasal and Raja Dhale also led to the term 'Dalit' being commonly used not just in Maharashtra but all over India.[17]

The Government of British India carved a new identity called the 'Scheduled Castes' for the untouchable castes, as they were put in a schedule (list) for providing constitutional safeguards to them under the new constitution of the British Government in India, 1937.

Though this term has been used in the present Constitution of the Republic of India, it does not contain any specific definition. Article 341 of the Constitution enjoins:

- The President of India may with respect to any state or union territory, and where it is a state, after consultation with the Governor thereof, by public notification, specify the castes, races or tribes, which shall for the purposes of this constitution be deemed to be scheduled castes in relation to that State or Union Territory, as the case may be.
- Parliament may by law include in or exclude from the list of scheduled castes specified in a notification issued under clause (1) any caste, race or tribe or part of group within any caste, race or tribe, but save as aforesaid a notification issued under the said clause shall not be varied by any subsequent notification.

Thus, the term 'scheduled caste' has become the constitutional identity for Dalits today.

Interestingly, the word 'Dalit' was first used in the context of caste oppression by Jyotiba Phule in the nineteenth century. Then, of course, Ambedkar used it extensively as well. Later, the Mahar community began to be known as Dalits, and soon after, the scheduled castes communities were referred to as Dalits—the credit for which is due to the Dalit Panthers movement.

Anand Teltumbde, an eminent Dalit academic, has explained the import of the term 'Dalit' and how it began to resonate all over India, like in Punjab, Uttar Pradesh and Tamil Nadu, as Dalits realised the need to form a constituency of their own. This was integral to the overall goal of assertion. As the book *Dalit Literature and Criticism* says:

> Dalit, thus, is a political term, a quasi-class identity, devised during the Ambedkarite movement, distinct from meaning 'Untouchable' and from the inert administrative labels 'Depressed Classes', 'Scheduled Castes' and certainly from Gandhi's patronizing 'Harijans'. The terms 'Dalit' reflected Ambedkar's aspiration that all the Untouchable castes would wear this new identity and form a formidable 'Dalit' constituency. Therefore

it was adopted by All Ambedkarite Dalits, initially the Mahars
in Maharashtra and slowly thereafter by the most populous and
dominant Dalit castes in other states like Punjab, UP, Tamil
Nadu.[18]

Under the leadership of Kanshiram, the Backward and Minority
Community Employees Federation (BAMCEF) propagated the
term 'Bahujan' as a class identity. Bahujan includes the scheduled
castes, scheduled tribes, other backward classes and minorities
such as Sikhs, Christians and Muslims. BAMCEF has also started
propagating Moolnivasi as an alternative identity to Dalits and
other backward castes.

When the Constitution came into force on 26 January 1950,
it was the beginning of a wonderful chapter in the history of India.
The Constitution, in effect, is a product of our ethos, aspirations
and political outlook combined. One of its most heartening aspects
was the public accepting the Constitution in full, especially with
respect to the affirmative measures incorporated for the Dalits.
The blacks in America had to relentlessly fight for years even after
the promulgation of the American constitution. But in India, it is
because of the vision of the founding members of the Constituent
Assembly, such as Babasaheb Ambedkar and Dakshayani
Velayudhan, that the principles of one man, one vote and same
value were accepted without any differences.

In the 1990s, the National Commission for Scheduled
Castes and Scheduled Tribes was set up under the constitutional
provisions, especially to look into their grievances and suggest
measures to offer them statutory protection from exploitation
and atrocities. Later, this body was bifurcated into the National
Commission for Scheduled Castes and the National Commission
for Scheduled Tribes. Article 17 abolished untouchability, and its
practice in any form was forbidden.

As per the 2011 Census,[19] the Dalit population comprises
16.6 per cent of the country's population. Punjab has the largest

Dalit population, close to 30 per cent of its population. States such as Bihar, West Bengal, Tamil Nadu, Uttar Pradesh and Andhra Pradesh constitute around 60 per cent of the total population of scheduled castes in the country.

Contemporary Dalit Discourse and the Quest for Social Democracy

Contemporary Dalit discourse is largely centred on one individual—B.R. Ambedkar. Needless to say, the nation as a whole has firm belief in his contributions as the leader of the depressed classes, the chief architect of the Constitution and a rich repository of academic knowledge and spiritual wisdom. After his death in 1956, there has been a huge transformation in Dalit imagination. Dalits are no longer silent about being considered a mere vote bank and now seek their denied rights and want to be instated as a thought bank. The scholarship around Dalit issues has rightly been focused on the ideas and propositions of Ambedkar, which still inspire the present-day generation of Dalit youth.

Social democracy is central to Ambedkar's philosophy and struggle. This is what distinguished him from the rest of the Indian freedom thinkers and fighters, who were struggling primarily for the liberation of the country (political freedom) from the yoke of the British Empire.

Ambedkar defined social democracy as:

A way of life which recognises liberty, equality and fraternity as the principles of life. These principles are not to be treated as separate items in a trinity. They form a union of trinity in the sense that to divorce one from the other is to defeat the very purpose of democracy.[20]

In fact, Ambedkar forewarned about the completion of the draft constitution in the Constituent Assembly on 25 November 1949:

On the 26th January 1950, we are going to enter into a life of contradictions. In politics we will have equality and in social and economic life we will have inequality. In politics we will be recognising the principle of one man one vote and one vote one value. In our social and economic life, we shall, by reason of our social and economic structure, continue to deny the principle of one man one value. How long shall we continue to live this life of contradictions? How long shall we continue to deny equality in our social and economic life? If we continue to deny it for long, we will do so only by putting our political democracy in peril. We must remove this contradiction at the earliest possible or else those who suffer from inequality will blow up the structure of political democracy which this Assembly has so laboriously built up.[21]

These words of Ambedkar mirror the words of Martin Luther King Jr, who, in his iconic 'I have a dream'[22] speech, made it clear that the time had come for the blacks to reclaim their right to life, liberty and happiness. Speaking from the steps of the Lincoln Memorial in Washington D.C. to a crowd of 200,000 or more, the speech was the culmination of a great march for justice and the greatest oration of all time.

In his words:

When the architects of our republic wrote the magnificent words of the Constitution and the Declaration of Independence, they were signing a promissory note to which every American was to fall heir. This note was a promise that all men, yes, black men as well as white men, would be guaranteed the inalienable rights of life, liberty, and the pursuit of happiness. It is obvious today that America has defaulted on this promissory note insofar as her citizens of color are concerned. Instead of honouring this sacred obligation, America has given the Negro people a bad check, which has come back marked 'insufficient funds'.

But we refuse to believe that the bank of justice is bankrupt. We refuse to believe that there are insufficient funds in the great vaults of opportunity of this nation. So we have come to cash this check—a check that will give us upon demand the riches of freedom and the security of justice.

The pristine vision of Ambedkar's social democracy was enshrined in the Constitution, which guaranteed certain fundamental rights to the citizens of India and enunciated certain directive principles of State policy, in particular, that the State would strive to promote the welfare of the people by securing and protecting as effectively as it may an order in which justice—social, economic and political— would inform all the institutions of national life, and would direct its policy towards securing, among other things:[23]

- That the citizens, men and women equally, have the right to an adequate means of livelihood.
- That the ownership and control of the material resources of the community are so distributed as best to subserve the common good.
- That the operation of the economic system does not result in the concentration of wealth and means of production to the common detriment.

Along with reservations in education, employment and legislature, some of the significant state initiatives taken over the past six decades since Independence are rural development programmes, public distribution systems, public health programmes, cooperatives, the Right to Education Act and the midday meals programme, which have helped social democracy in India. Thus, as former prime minister Manmohan Singh said, the Constitution of India is 'a unique social charter—the boldest statement ever of social democracy'.[24] However, whether these varied measures have been able to facilitate the growth of social democracy in India is a matter of debate and contention. Nevertheless, the incorporation of such measures in the Constitution is vindication enough that the founding fathers of independent India wanted to deepen the roots of liberal democracy while placing it on a firm foundation of social democracy.

In that way, we are clear that the caste system has to go and there is no alternative to social reformation. We understand that this is a sensitive subject but if reformation of our society is the need of the hour, then the onus is on us—we, the people. We must reform in keeping with the times—this is our unequivocal view. There are many reformers, such as Ambedkar, Ram Manohar Lohia and Veer Savarkar, who tried their best to weed out caste. This important churn must restart. Caste and untouchability must have no place in our lexicon—be it in thought, word or deed.

The deep malice towards caste and the sheer ignorance of the need to eradicate it can be traced back to pre-Independence days, to the then political leadership. During the first three decades of its existence, the Indian National Congress (INC) did not pass any resolution emphasizing to their fellow countrymen or to the British Indian government the need to remove the social evils arising from the caste system, and its rituals, traditions and usage.

'I understand democracy as something that would give the weak the same chance as the strong,'[25] Mahatma Gandhi had said. But even after seventy years of Independence, Dalits continue their battle of right to dignity because the thought that another human being's touch can pollute you exists even today. With the unfortunate suicide of Rohith Vemula at Hyderabad Central University, there has been a build-up of a national-level narrative around the issues and concerns of the Dalit community. Be it Una or Bhima Koregaon, violence against Dalits in India is again in the spotlight.

Even today, Dalits cannot enter a house by the main door, they cannot drink tea in a local tea shop, and Dalit children cannot sit with non-Dalit ones. Incidents of rape, physical assault and murder are rampant in both rural and urban pockets of the country. Such incidents, in particular, are grave when it comes to Dalits. The National Crime Records Bureau (NCRB) published by the Ministry of Home Affairs states that there has been a 66 per cent increase in cases of caste-related atrocities between 2007 and 2017.[26]

In fact, as we write this introduction, a common friend has put up a post on social media that perhaps gives a perspective to the deeper malice that exists today and makes our heads hang in shame:

> People say caste system doesn't exist any longer. Let me tell you I was out on a dinner with an extremely educated guy and we were talking about life and different perspectives and my everyday struggles being a woman, and that man says something to me that completely shakes me. He says that if a boy from an upper caste marries me (a Dalit) he will do me a great favour as society considers me to be a low born. With tears in my eyes, I left the dinner table.[27]

As per an analysis of the 2012 India Human Development Survey, 27 per cent of the households in India practised untouchability, in which the practice was more prevalent in rural areas, at 30 per cent, and urban areas, at 20 per cent.[28] Caste rigidity in marriage continues to be deeply entrenched. While there is no accurate data available, people continue to marry within their own caste/community.[29] A telephonic survey[30] conducted by four professors over 40,000 households in six states, published in the *Economic and Political Weekly* (EPW) in 2016, found untouchability the highest in rural Rajasthan, where 66 per cent of non-Dalit women and 50 per cent of non-Dalit men admitted to the practice. When they were asked if they wanted a law to ban inter-caste marriages, more than half agreed.

In 2017, a study[31] of 6000 people between the ages of fifteen and thirty-four—conducted by the Centre for the Study of

Developing Societies (CSDS) and Konrad-Adenauer-Stiftung—showed that graduate Dalits faced the highest frequency of caste discrimination among social groups. Young Dalit graduates often face discrimination while appearing for their first job interview. In 2007, professors Sukhadeo Thorat and Paul Attewell found that young Dalits stood a significantly less chance of being called for an interview in comparison to equally qualified general-category candidates.[32]

There are even several prohibitions that Dalits have been subjected to—such as no driving through a locality, even in their own vehicle, no taking their deceased from the main streets of the village, especially where upper castes live, no mounting a horse at a wedding procession, no entering a higher-caste locality for wedding functions, and no playing musical instruments for their weddings.

According to a report published by the National Human Rights Commission (NHRC) in 2010 on the prevention of atrocities against scheduled castes and scheduled tribes, 'A crime is committed against a Dalit once in every 18 minutes. Every day, on average, three Dalit women are raped, two Dalits murdered, and two Dalit houses burnt.'[33] The report further details categories of exclusion and the different forms of discrimination. It also highlights the fact that Dalits do not have access to community sources of water and other public services on account of the scourge of 'untouchability' that persists in society despite it being abolished in 1956 and being unlawful today.

Over the decades leading up to 2016, the crime rate against Dalits rose by 25 per cent—from 16.3 crimes per 100,000 Dalits reported in 2006 to 20.3 crimes in 2016—according to an IndiaSpend analysis of 2016 NCRB data.[34] The analysis further added that the cases pending police investigation for both marginalized groups had risen by 99 per cent and 55 per cent, respectively, while the pendency in courts had risen by 50 per cent and 28 per cent, respectively. The conviction rates for crime against scheduled castes and scheduled tribes had fallen by 2 percentage points and 7 percentage points, respectively, to 26 per cent and 21 per cent from 2006 to 2016. In total, there have been as many as 422,799 recorded crimes against Dalits or scheduled castes. The highest increase in the rate of crime was recorded in eight states—Goa, Kerala, Delhi, Gujarat, Bihar, Maharashtra, Jharkhand and Sikkim—where it increased more than tenfold.

In the recent past, Dalit weddings have been interrupted by upper castes in Rajasthan, Uttar Pradesh and Gujarat. In April 2018, in Uttar Pradesh, a Dalit, Sanjay Jatav,[35] was denied the right to ride a mare to his wedding. When he protested, water and electricity supply to his and his fiancée's family were stopped by upper-caste families. In 2018, a twenty-one-year-old Dalit, Pradip Rathod,[36] was allegedly killed in Gujarat by upper-caste men for owning and riding a horse. The Dalit community in Gujarat has also been assaulted for sporting a moustache and performing garba, the popular Gujarati folk dance.

In Dhuwaliya village, in Rajasthan's Bhilwara district, Prakash Meghwanshi's wedding procession, or bindauli, as the procession is locally called, was stopped by a group of upper-caste men and women, who asked him to get off his horse in front of the houses of the upper caste residents. Meghwanshi refused, and only when his family threatened to call the police was the procession allowed to pass.[37]

In Tamil Nadu, Dalit women in panchayat politics have to negotiate three kinds of oppression—rigid caste structures within the village, patriarchy within and without their families, and feudalism, where they are in a dependent economic relationship with the dominant caste in the village.

In incidents that can only be termed bizarre, genuine representation of Dalits in the field of politics has been curtailed. A village in Madurai, Kodikulam, auctioned off its president, a poor, illiterate Dalit woman whom the villagers had been forced to elect because the post had been reserved for a Dalit woman.[38]

Despite her pleas that she would hand over all her 'earnings' to the village committee, Balamani Veeman, the panchayat president, was auctioned off. And this was not a one-off incident. The practice first came to light in 2001, when it was reported that panchayat posts were being 'auctioned' off and Dalits were being prevented from filing nominations in villages.

To this day, it is impossible to see reasonable representation of subaltern voices in newsrooms. Kenneth J. Cooper from the *Washington Post* was the first to direct national attention to this issue in 1996, when he found that there was not a single Dalit journalist in India.[39] This prompted another senior journalist, B.K. Uniyal from the *Pioneer*, to do similar research.[40] Of 700 accredited journalists, not a single Dalit was found.

Having said that, on the ground, Dalits are questioning the status quo in significant ways. The Bharat bandh called by various organizations and Dalit groups on 2 April 2018 was representative of a social churning taking place in Dalit society. Caste-based conversations have always formed the cornerstone of our society. We only fool ourselves by saying that caste is not a reality, when, in reality, it has only grown stronger in the institution of marriage and other social interactions.

Bihar, Punjab, Uttar Pradesh and Maharashtra have witnessed demonstrations seeking a review of the apex court order towards the dilution of the Scheduled Castes and the Scheduled Tribes (Prevention of Atrocities) Act, 1989. Debate on this Act is not new.

Dalits have traditionally been dispossessed of land and related assets, and this has been attributed to their inferior status in society. Caste is very much linked to the skewed distribution of land to the Dalits. It is also believed that Ambedkar realized this from the very beginning of his struggle and therefore initiated several land struggles in Maharashtra. Dada Saheb Gaikwad, an Ambedkarite, was instrumental in leading countrywide land struggles.

Importance of Land to Dalits

In his book *DNA of Dalit Movement*, Ojha Jai Prakash details the pattern of how Dalits were deprived of land. He writes:

> If we take a look at the reports of National Campaign on Dalit Human Rights 2006. From 1948 to 1970s, 340 million hectares of land were given to the farmers, out of which only 0.5 percent was given to the schedule castes and tribes. In addition, the report also points out that out of an estimated 30 million hectares of harvestable surplus land, only 7.5 million hectares have been declared surplus and only a small portion of it has gone to the Dalits.[41]

The scenario today has not changed much—while a majority of Indian farmers grow on their own land, Dalit farmers in much of the country continue to work for wages, as per the latest Census of India data. The census divides farmers into two categories—cultivators, who have an ownership stake in the land, and agricultural labourers, who work for wages on land that they do not own. Dalit farmers are more likely than other farmers to work for wages, according to census data from 2011. In states with histories of feudalism, Dalits are much more likely to work as agricultural labourers. In Bihar, Haryana, Punjab, Gujarat, Andhra Pradesh, Tamil Nadu and Kerala, nearly all Dalit farmers are agricultural labourers. In most districts, the figure is above 90 per cent.[42]

Suraj Yengde, who is with the Department of African and African American Studies at Harvard and is also a W.E.B. Du Bois non-resident fellow, says Dalits should never cease to assert their right to land. In one of his weekly columns for *Hindustan Times*, he wrote,

> The landownership for the community is the lowest in the country. Only 9.23% land is owned by Dalits, according to the

NSSO Household Ownership and Operational Holdings in India. Dalits have to become much fiercer in their demand for land. Since they don't own land, they have no place to call their own. Because of this caste India becomes a confused space to articulate genuine critical conversations around Dalit existence.[43]

Another statistic related to this is that at the all-India level, according to the National Sample Survey Office (66th round) survey, the proportion of rural scheduled caste households 'self-employed in agriculture', that is, having their own land, is only 17.1 per cent, compared with the 39.4 per cent among rural households of the socially advanced classes (SACs).[44]

Pertinent to note here is that mainstream movies today highlight this aspect of land dispossession in the Dalits and the caste-based discrimination and violence that follow as a result. One such recent example is *Asuran*, a Tamil film starring Dhanush, which released on 4 October 2019 and became his biggest hit. It also became the highest grossing Indian film at the Malaysian box office this year, beating the Bollywood multistarrer *War*.

Asuran is the story of Sivasamy (Dhanush), a Dalit man who avenges the death of his family members, who are victims of caste-based violence. Based on Sahitya Akademi award winner Poomani's novel *Vekkai*, the movie deals with panchami land rights—the land given by the British to the scheduled castes, which cannot be transferred to others.

The subject of giving land to Dalits or solving the problem of Dalit landlessness is not new or recent.

The problem of Dalits dispossessed of land is attributed to them being prohibited and prevented from owning land, not just because of untouchability but also by formal laws such as the Punjab Agricultural Land Alienation Act, 1901, of the larger pre-Partition Punjab. This Act inter alia wrongly classified the two most populous Dalit agricultural labour communities as non-agricultural and made them statutorily ineligible to own land.[45]

As a possible solution to land issues faced by Dalits, former bureaucrats like the late P.S. Krishnan consistently suggested to governments to undertake a centrally funded national crash programme to distribute all available government land to all rural Dalit families and land-deprived tribal families, along with other rural landless agricultural labour families, mainly belonging to the SEdBCs (socially and educationally backward classes). He added that some of these government lands would need reclamation, for which technology was available and the required labour input could be secured purposefully through MGNREGA (Mahatma Gandhi National Rural Employment Guarantee Act). In fact, he also established that there was adequate land not only for all rural scheduled caste families but also for non-Dalit rural landless agricultural labour families.[46]

Channelling Dalit Assertion to Seek Representation

Today, there is a significant churn that can be witnessed in the Dalit community to move from isolation to assertion. One must bear in mind that this change has come about because of the contribution of several religious reformers, revolutionaries and sociopolitical activists and because of the increase in caste-related crimes. In addition, several community organizations continue to work for mobilization and emancipatory assertion. It would be safe to say that Dalit assertion has grown from local to national to global levels.

Ram Madhav, former member of the board of governors, India Foundation, put this assertion into context in one of his columns. Writing for the *Indian Express*, he said,

In the mid-1990s, a Dalit sub-caste in Andhra Pradesh started using their caste name as a suffix to their names. This, in their view, was a proud assertion of their identity. This act led to serious discussion among the intelligentsia. Many were worried that casteism was staging a comeback. But a simple and profound question asked by a Dalit intellectual put the discussion to rest. In Andhra, people belonging to several non-Dalit castes use their caste name as a suffix. This has been the practice for long. Never did the question of growing casteism arise when Sharma or Shastry or Reddy was used as a suffix. Why this concern when a Dalit does the same?[47]

Also, to understand this Dalit assertion, it is important that one first understands the objective behind it. The Dalit society, movement and icons have a much larger agenda of nation-building than what has been highlighted.

In fact, author Mohan Dass Namishray goes on to explain the phenomenon of Dalit assertion in the 1857 revolt in detail. He writes,

A fortnightly newspaper, *Dalit Kesari*, published a special issue on the 1857 revolt of Indian Independence, in which the lead article was on Matadin Bhangi. This described Bhangi as the pioneer of the First War of Independence. In fact two other publications, *Anarya Bharat*, published from UP, and *Himayati*, a Dalit literary magazine, have also had lead articles of the contribution of Matadin Bhangi. But unfortunately historians have forgotten his contribution.[48]

Namishray adds details on several Dalit icons, such as Chetram Jatav, Balluram Mehtar, Banke Chamar and Vira Pasi, who were all martyred in the 1857 revolt. Namshray explains:

Although the Dalits were born in the lowest caste of the Indian caste hierarchy and suffered great hardship because of their poor socio-economic status, they never sold the interests of their country for their own benefit. No one can accuse a single Dalit of doing so. Whenever the need arose, they sacrificed their lives for their motherland. Among the brave sons of the country, the names of Matadin Bhangi, Balluram Mehtrar and Chetram Jatav are written in shining letters.[49]

True to this, the inherent interest, passion and willingness of the Dalits to be associated with the Indian armed forces caught our attention; and we found that this phenomenon was not just restricted to the First War of Independence in 1857. Kautilya, in his Arthashastra, advocates for Dalits, then Sudras, to join the armed forces. In the case of Ambedkar, his own father was in the armed forces; in fact, Ambedkar's impending wish was to write a book on the history of the Indian Army. Udham Singh, to make ends meet, enrolled in the then British armed forces. Therefore, the passion of Dalits to be associated with the armed forces is evidenced right from ancient Indian texts like the Arthashastra.[50]

Dalits today seek representation at the institutions of governance and the highest echelons of power, from the local three-tier Panchayati Raj Institution, to being members of the legislative assembly and the Parliament. Dalits today seek to actively shape identities at national and international levels.

Professor Vivek Kumar of Jawaharlal Nehru University, Delhi, in his book *Roaring Revolution: Dalit Assertion and New Horizon,* notes:

Dalit assertion is a roaring revolution rather than a silent revolution and this is taking place in almost all aspects of the Indian society today. Dalit assertion started with certain conscious individuals for their own emancipation. Hence we found Ravidasis (followers of Guru Ravidas), Kabirpanthees (followers of Kabir), in the medieval period revering their teachers and asserting their rights. Similarly in the 19th century number of socio-political organisations emerged in almost every nook and corner of the country. The objective of these organisations was to demand legitimate human rights—

economic, religious, educational and political, which were a
prerequisite for a dignified living.[51]

This Dalit assertion seeks to claim rights for their women, youth,
intellectuals, bureaucrats, diaspora and NGOs. It is interesting to
note, though, that this Dalit assertion exclusively through political
demands came only in the 1930s led by Ambedkar and later
through the works of Kanshiram. Ambedkar favoured political
reforms in addition to social reforms because he realized that the
latter alone would not lead to Dalit empowerment. There are
a couple of case studies that put this in perspective—one is the
coming to the fore of Ambedkar's Independent Labour Party and
BAMCEF.

Ambedkar participated in the Round Table Conferences in
1932 between the British government and the INC, and demanded
equal political rights for Dalits. It is because of these demands
that he, on 15 August 1936, established the Independent Labour
Party, the first political party established by Dalits.

Ambedkar also believed that education was a powerful
weapon for the community to assert itself. However, in this, he
could have been said to be carrying forward the legacy of Savitribai
Phule, who, in essence, stood for the importance of education
in the emancipation of Dalits. As a firm believer in knowledge,
Ambedkar coined the slogan 'Educate, Organize and Agitate'.
He also established the People's Education Society in erstwhile
Bombay in 1945. This society, in turn, set up a number of colleges
and schools in Bombay and Aurangabad in Maharashtra to provide
modern and non-discriminatory education to Dalits. Ambedkar's
efforts saw results when many Dalit youth took to education as an
important tool of self-empowerment.

Ambedkar's efforts towards the framing of the Constitution
cannot be stressed enough. The Constituent Assembly worked for
two years, eleven months and seventeen days since it first met on 9
December 1946. Ambedkar was present on all days and the initial

draft of the Constitution contained 243 Articles and 13 Schedules. In its final form, the draft Constitution contained 395 Articles and 8 Schedules.

The Bahujan movement initiated by Kanshiram was a reaction to the regressive practice of treating Dalits as a political commodity. He led one of the most successful non-political movements to consolidate Dalits through BAMCEF. The outfit was conceived to address social inequalities of caste, gender and community. Kanshiram galvanized this social coalition and gave it political shape in the form of the Bahujan Samaj Party (BSP), which became the pre-eminent Dalit voice in national politics. He nurtured Mayawati politically to ensure the movement continued after him.

Apart from the emergence of the BSP and BAMCEF, more than a dozen parties have been established by Dalits, like the Scheduled Castes Federation (1942), which eventually led to the formation of the Republican Party of India (1957), the Dalit Panthers (1972), the Lok Janshakti Party (2000), the Dalit Panthers of India (1990s) and the Puthiya Tamizhagam (1990s). All of these parties have had some impact or the other on Indian politics, but it is the BSP that has been the most successful.

The nation has seen a Dalit president (K.R. Narayanan), a Dalit deputy prime minister (Babu Jagjivan Ram), a Dalit Lok Sabha Speaker (G.M.C. Balayogi) and several Dalit vice-chancellors, professors, thinkers, bureaucrats, leaders and intellectuals. If we delve deeper, we will find that our history is filled with examples of heroes from disadvantaged backgrounds who have persevered to perpetuate our civilizational core.

Over the decade leading up to 2011, the literacy rate among India's Dalits grew faster than that of the general population. For scheduled castes, it grew 11.4 percentage points, from 54.7 per cent to 66.1 per cent, compared to an increase of 8.2 percentage points, from 64.8 per cent to 73 per cent, for India's general population.[52]

In fact, in Madhya Pradesh's last *gram* panchayat elections, which took place in 2014–15, the candidates for the post of sarpanch (village head) from the scheduled castes, scheduled tribes and other backward classes won more than 18,183 seats, more than 80 per cent of the total 22,604 seats. Only 15,136 seats— about 67 per cent of the total seats—were reserved for candidates of these communities.

The results of the assembly elections in Uttar Pradesh, held in 2017, had a tremendous implication for subaltern politics in the country. The verdict delivered a body blow to those who claimed to represent the cause of the marginalized. It shocked the intelligentsia, which refused to acknowledge the presence of multiple perspectives. A striking feature of Uttar Pradesh, one of India's most politically significant states, is the changing voting dynamics of the Dalit community. BJP candidates won in seventy-five out of eighty-five assembly constituencies reserved for scheduled caste candidates.

Milind Kamble, who fought social barriers and created Dalit Indian Chamber of Commerce & Industry (DICCI)—a platform for grooming Dalit entrepreneurs—is an inspiration. As is Arjun Meghwal, who rose from being a telephone operator to a minister in the Union Cabinet. As authors, we also take inspiration from Tina Dabi, the first Dalit woman to top the UPSC examination. Not to mention filmmakers such as Pa. Ranjith and Mari Selvaraj, who used the Tamil films *Kabali* and *Pariyerum Perumal* as vehicles to convey the sociopolitical message of Dalit-led empowerment.

The installation of statues of Dalit personalities at public places has helped the general public develop an understanding of Dalit aspirations and history. Renaming roads and districts after Dalit icons has also instilled a sense of pride and self-respect in the overall Dalit population. India has also seen several social reformers, such as Sri Ramanujacharya, Kabir Das and Namdev, who were consistent in creating a philosophical foundation for social cohesion. What was significant was this brought a sense of pride and dignity to the Dalits and encouraged their participation and representation in public life. These reformers were relentless in awakening the masses to the ills of caste discrimination, and enabled reorganization and reinvention of society. Their underlying message was not just self-respect but a dignified living for all.

Swami Vivekananda spoke beautifully of Sri Ramanujacharya. In his words,

> Sri Ramanujacharya's was a large heart who cried for the downtrodden at a time when being downtrodden was recognized and accepted as part of one's karma. He broke the settled prejudice of his times.[53]

Sri Ramanujacharya foresaw, a thousand years before, the hidden and unspoken aspirations of the downtrodden. He realized the need to include the socially excluded and the outcaste, to make not only religion but society itself holistic.

Ambedkar dedicated his book *The Untouchables*[54] to three Dalit saints—Nandanar (Tamil Nadu), Guru Ravidas (Uttar Pradesh) and Chokha Mela (Maharashtra). In one of his writings on Sri Ramanujacharya, Ambedkar praised him for his relentless contribution to Hinduism and for working towards a cohesive society. According to Ambedkar, Ramanujacharya accepted a Dalit as his guru; this sent a strong message to society about integration being the sole way forward.

There is another interesting anecdote to corroborate this point. There is a small village, Vadhu Budruk, near Pune, where a memorial of Sambhaji stands tall alongside a samadhi of Govind Gopal Gaikwad. After Sambhaji, son of Chhatrapati Shivaji, was assassinated by Aurangzeb, his body mutilated and thrown into the river, it was Gaikwad, a Mahar from the village, who collected the parts of his body, stitched them together and conducted his last rites. It was inspirational and paved the way for integration and social unity. There are multiple such examples in Indian history that bolster the inevitability of an inclusive society.

Accusations targeting any one political party or ideology for an increase in cases of caste atrocity are misleading. One can gauge the magnitude of such atrocities without relying on any agenda-driven propaganda. A simple Internet search on the word 'Dalit' will expose readers to the monstrous levels of atrocity committed against people from the socially deprived segments of society.

There can be multiple hypotheses around why there's rising Dalit assertion in India today. Commentators, according to their respective understandings and affiliations, view this as either aspirational or rebellious. The makers of modern discourse have been toying with the idea of what a new Dalit narrative should be like. What would constitute the central theme of the emerging Dalit discourse? And who will be the real stakeholders defining the twenty-first-century Dalit chronicle?

During the country's presidential elections between Ram Nath Kovind and Meira Kumar, Sanjay Paswan, Bihar's member of legislative council and former Central minister, quipped, 'Thanks to Dalit movements and social media campaigns, Dalits have become the centre of discourse now. No political party, including the BJP, can ignore Dalits. In fact, this presidential election is a victory of Dalit movements in the country.'[55]

It becomes pertinent here to acknowledge the services of DICCI, a unique conglomerate of Dalit entrepreneurs across the nation, which has more than 5,000 big and small names as its members. The Union government under Prime Minister Narendra Modi has also launched schemes such as Stand-Up India, which focuses on creating a supportive ecosystem for aspiring Dalit entrepreneurs. More than 125,000 branches of public-sector banks have been mandated to extend financial support to entrepreneurs from the scheduled castes and scheduled tribes.[56]

In addition to preaching the teachings of Ambedkar, the lessons of leaders such as Kanshiram and India's former deputy prime minister Jagjivan Ram must be acknowledged today.

The current prime minister and president of India, Narendra Modi and Ram Nath Kovind, respectively, come from humble backgrounds. They are aware of the pain, agony, challenges, deprivations and everyday threats that a socially disadvantaged person faces in the rural set-up. Under Modi's leadership, the Parliament has discussed the life and works of Ambedkar, and the BJP currently has fifty-two Dalit MPs in the 17th Lok Sabha.

As researchers, we felt that it was essential to undertake this project, because even though our nation has seen great progress and development, it is apparent that the contribution of Dalits has been neglected by the academia, thinkers and policymakers, and in more subtle ways than are expressed in day-to-day life. While caste discrimination still largely remains a stain on this country, whether looked at from the inside or the outside, little effort has been made to even blur the caste lines, let alone eliminate them altogether.

There's also a certain confusion that exists, because it is discrimination in thought, word and deed that has to be removed, not the characterizations that define our beautiful and diverse culture. We need to have a clear understanding of how we want to move ahead as a nation. The mood today is one of indifference and apathy, outside and often even within Dalit communities. For many, this is an attempt to escape the trauma of the past, for others it is an embarrassment, victimhood or a myriad of other feelings. For such people, this book, which presents victors that have risen up from positions of disadvantage, will serve as a medal of achievement and honour.

Even today, representation remains elusive in key spheres for Dalits. The Dalit youth today feels that the Dalit worldview is still a 'work in progress'. Confrontation is not the answer, but the need of the hour is a constructive path that leads to collaboration.

The community must be equipped with skills to negotiate with the administration. It is time to shift the focus from emotive rhetoric to an agenda of empowerment. Dalits seek jobs and a better life in metropolitan cities. Therefore, it is imperative that individuals and organizations working towards Dalit emancipation and empowerment also realize that the need is to go beyond 'sitting, eating, meeting' gestures and free Dalits from 'vote bank' tags.

In the words of Malcolm X, 'Let the black man speak his mind so that the white man really knows how he feels. Once you put the facts on the table, it's possible to arrive at a solution.'[57] Through this introduction, we also wish to advocate for a proposal on Dalit issues that would encapsulate the scale and magnitude of atrocities, the impact of welfare and punitive legislations, and how distributive the policies of affirmative action have been for the deprived segment of our society. The present need is to depoliticize the Dalit discourse and strive towards an independent, objective, dispassionate and solution-centric Dalit narrative.

The Premise: Deconstructing History

Makers of Modern Dalit History is not just for a Dalit readership. It is a collection of profiles on role models that we should all know about, and know well. Each citizen of this country has a role to play in its future. When you know a nation's history, you become a solution—qualified to look ahead to a brighter and better future.

It is our hope that this book will enable communities to get together and focus on the nation as one entity without losing their own distinct uniqueness. The most important consideration is focus. The profiles in this book describe heroes who overlooked personal hardships to make a mark—and what a mark indeed. They are sources of inspiration and optimism. These are stories that have universal and timeless appeal. Each of these personalities signifies the very premise of the idea of India. In each of the times that they lived in, they shaped generations and showed the way for future generations to observe, emulate and aspire for a cohesive society. They have created a unique identity and pride of place not just for themselves, but for the communities they hailed from, and for the wider community that simply considers itself Indians first.

Journalism has a principal rule for reporting, namely the 5W's and 1H (What, When, Where, Why, Who and How). This rule applies even today when contextualizing history anywhere in the world. Through *Makers of Modern Dalit History*, we have attempted to revise history keeping this rule in mind, and in the process have also underscored the relevance of these heroes for today's readers.

There are several case studies of not just documenting but reinterpreting history worldwide. In the United States, there is an organization called the Organization of American Historians, which was started with a commitment to studying and teaching the history of America. A key mission of the organization is to promote scholarship in the presentation of American history.

British philosopher Karl Popper succinctly put forth his perspective on the need to reinterpet history in one's own way, because each generation will have its own point of view. 'Each generation has its own troubles and problems, and, therefore, its own interests and its own point of view, and that, it follows that each generation has a right to look upon and re-interpret history in their own way,' he said.[58]

This is a significant reason to why we felt it was important to write about each of these subaltern personalities, who stand for diversity in unity.

As the authors of this book, we have wondered why the accounts of these important makers of history do not feature in the written accounts we have available—and even if they do, why there's hardly anything of substance about them. This is our attempt to reverse these omissions. These are contributions that cannot be missed. These stories have to be told and retold until they are part of popular culture. When these pillars of society stand tall and gain greater visibility, they will allow us a wider vision of our past and our future, and instil a sense of pride in our youth. Each reader will find something to relate to in this book. The profiles, both male and female, span all parts of India and various periods in time—from the patriotism of Udham Singh, Rani Jhalkaribai, Gurram Jashuva to the contribution via governance and polity of heroes such as K.R. Narayanan, Dakshayani Velayudhan, Babu Jagjivan Ram, Kanshiram and Jogendranath Mandal; from the social reforms brought about by great visionaries such as Babasaheb Ambedkar and Ayyankali to the creative brilliance of poets and seers such as Guru Ravidas and Kabir Das; from the tireless work in the area of gender justice and education by Savitribai Phule to the transformation via spiritual ideas by Veda Vyasa, Valmiki and Nandanar; not to mention the pure example set by the values and virtues of devotee-saints like Janabai and Soyarabai.

Why These Individuals?

Much thought has gone into the selection of these Dalit icons based on how they have impacted society. This is not an academic exercise, and the aim is not to just educate people about the lives of these people who have not been given their due in history. This book has allowed us, the authors, to ponder on their contributions and internalize them. If the readers connect in the same way and understand the values that prompted the selfless vision of these Dalit heroes, the objective of writing this book would have been fulfilled.

For instance, whatever's written or said about Bharat Ratna awardee B.R. Ambedkar would be inadequate to describe his contribution, not just to the Dalit discourse, but to the entire nation. He was a multi-faceted personality with brilliant ideas of unity. He went beyond his call of duty and expanded the reach of his work and contribution to benefit all communities.

One of the profiles of the book outlines the sheer grit of Udham Singh, whose entire adult life was dedicated to avenging the Jallianwala Bagh massacre. Udham Singh was not a defeatist. He did not sit back and accept the insult and injury experienced by his people by the hands of the British Raj. In a selfless and devoted act of requiting its people, his rage transformed into resolve.

Today, India is greatly benefitting in many ways from the ancient poet sage Veda Vyasa's systematic thought process and tireless efforts. He constantly questioned his own self and came up with refreshing and truly unstoppable ways to reach people. In Vyasa's work one can find technique, plot development, character portrayal, description of nature seamlessly coming together to weave tales and sometimes even form an effortless connection with culture.

Then there is India's first Dalit president, K.R. Narayanan who served office from 1997 till 2000. Narayanan was not just passionate about education but also had an all-inclusive, optimistic view of the country. He was known for putting his cause before himself. Finding a man of his genius, intellect and noble intent would be a tall order indeed, but it is not impossible. In the field of politics, K.R. Narayanan is a great example for emulation.

Sant Janabai's profile details the divinization of a difficult life and her story is one of tremendous inspiration. A disadvantaged orphan who was kept at a physical distance from her beloved deity Vitthala, Janabai held on to the purity of her feelings for the Lord that brought her closer than the closest to Him. Her compositions have had, and will continue to have, a huge impact on those who got familiar with her work. In a first, the company of saints, conferred upon her, the title of *Sant* (Dalit bhakti saint), in times when the epithet was been used only for males.

And wouldn't it be a matter of such pride if we Indians could display the values of Babu Jagjivan Ram, who met discrimination with excellence and achievement, choosing to build on the positives rather than running away from the negatives? He was a social worker, a grass-roots leader who had a subtle understanding of social structure, an erudite parliamentarian, an able administrator, a leader of the depressed classes and the Dalits, a father, and a cabinet minister, whose life contained invaluable and precious lessons.

Kabir Das is also profiled in the book. Seeking God within the self, as also in logic, devotion, reason, simplicity, and wisdom, this weaver-saint's prose and poetry are still as meaningful and relevant today as they were in his times. Kabir is a critical insider in the intellectual tradition of India, who critiqued purposeless rituals, sought for people to not limit themselves to the confines of caste and urged them to seek God in their own being.

It is crucial to include Jhalkaribai and her contribution during the first war of Independence in 1857. An astute strategist, an adviser of Rani Lakshmibai, and a fearless warrior, Rani Jhalkaribai was a force to reckon with. She represents the assertion and challenge that should be posed to orthodoxy and outdated ideas.

Kanshiram stands out as an example of smartness coupled with goodness and he had vision and nurtured the idea of inclusive leadership. In such a person, the scope for achievement is indeed unimaginable, and therefore, it was only but natural to include him in the profiles. A political pioneer, who was much ahead of his time, his main aim was to bring about social transformation with the political empowerment of Dalits. Kanshiram was also responsible for bringing to the fore legacies of Dalit cultural icons and heroes from the past, which can help galvanize the community.

All of us can only hope to have the audacity, integrity and dignity of someone like Dakshayani Velayudhan, who stood her ground in her toughest moments with her head held high. Acute discrimination did not deter Dakshayani, she questioned all social beliefs and norms, thereby developing a certain independence of thought and opinion. However, in spite of her achievements, many still do not know that this pathbreaker was the first Dalit woman graduate of India. Dakshayani also made history by being one of the 15 women members to be elected to the Constituent Assembly of India.

Most often Jogendranath Mandal is only remembered for his famous resignation letter that he tendered in Pakistan and returned to India. It is unfortunate that he is absent from the national story of India, Pakistan and Bangladesh. In this book, we showcase his efforts in the field of education, his advocacy of the idea of reservation for Dalits in co-operative departments, his means of facilitating Ambedkar's candidature from Bengal, and his effort to encourage Ambedkar to take on the task of drafting the Constitution of India.

It is one thing to speak of equality for all, but an entirely different thing to live that belief and to live its import, like Nandanar did. If a mind like B.R. Ambedkar was inspired by Nandanar, to whom he dedicated his book, then his mettle needs no more validity than that. Social reformers in Tamil Nadu, armed with determination and knowledge, have fought hard to rid the system of the evils of caste and caste-based discrimination. Nandanar is another gem in the treasure trove of the state's social reformers.

Ayyankali from Kerala is a great leader to emulate in this regard. One brilliant initiative of his was to use music and dance as part of a creative rebellion against caste-discrimination. In addition to this, Ayyankali took a stand for the principles of gender justice and advocated for the importance of education. Taking inspiration from his life elucidated in his profile, we can strive for affirmative action to uphold the dignity of the Dalits.

Another social reformer who used poetry as part of his creative rebellion is Andhra Pradesh's Gurram Jashuva. His poetry rose from the margins to make it to mainstream Telugu literature. Even today, it continues to permeate through the works of several writers, admirers and observers. A Padma Bhushan awardee, Jashuva was the only Dalit poet in Telugu whose writings are a part of curricular readings in high schools and universities of the state. Jashuva advocated for Dalits to take part in the anti-colonial struggle against the British and admired Vivekananda and Subhas Chandra Bose. Jashuva, through his writings, also questioned the orthodoxy, the learned and the saints' indifference to social reformation.

Another fascinating individual who has been profiled, is Soyarabai, wife of Chokha Mela. She is a wonderful role model for the women suffering social injustices who feel that they can make no difference in society. The values she embodies are relevant Indian society even today.

Others, like Guru Ravidas, a contemporary of Kabir Das, who was from the cobbler community, have met social injustice with a spiritual quest for freedom at the subtlest level. He uplifted the society by clearing the vision of the people who came in contact with him. He took tragedies in his stride and used peace as a weapon of social protest to fight false values.

Savitribai Phule is not just a woman but an institution in herself. Today, women's empowerment is a popular movement supported by many but more than a century before such terminology even existed, Savitribai changed the face of education for women in India. Today, Savitribai Phule is largely known only in Maharashtra, whereas she should be celebrated as a true hero and role model in every part of the nation.

Sage Valmiki, the first poet of India, was a dynamic storyteller who gave India some of its pioneering literary texts like the Ramayana and the Yoga Vasishta wherein he elucidated on the subtlest of human philosophies for the benefit of mankind.

The final chapter revolves around the lives of present-day Dalit icons who have overcome adversity to create their own unique identities—be it in art, academia, entrepreneurship, politics, education or sports—and continue in their pursuit as nation builders by inspiring thousands with their achievements.

Despite their restricted social mobility, all the Dalit icons profiled here have left an indelible mark on India's history.

These largely forgotten stalwarts have dedicated their lives to creating an equal platform for all citizens, irrespective of caste, creed and gender. What India needs today is to take a leaf from their books. While each incident written about in the book is inspiring, we encourage readers to also reflect on the underlying values that are presented here. If adopted by the citizens of today, these values will have far-reaching results in the character-building of our nation.

Our attempt is just a humble addition to the ever-evolving Dalit discourse. We are also not afraid of the criticism, if any, that the book may attract. We also know that the writings could be redundant to some and insightful to some others. We have tried to walk the tight rope by representing key moments in the lives of these icons and understanding their vision for Dalit-led empowerment. In essence, we have tried to remain true to the lives of these heroes.

Socio-economic disparity and income inequality are going to be huge challenges for the generations to come. No one must be denied the opportunity to access the benefits accruing from technological growth and advancement on the basis of their birth.

We hope that this treatise will be a positive intervention in the otherwise dominating pessimistic narrative around social justice. A comprehensive outlook, an informed perspective and an unbiased approach is what we want to achieve through our work.

Having seen from up close the struggle for survival of Dalits in various professional and academic ecosystems, we promise to present to the reader a world that is still evolving from ignorance, indignity, nervousness and agitation. Countless years of discrimination have left an indelible mark on the vision and imagination of the Dalits, often bringing the journey towards attaining self-confidence to a screeching halt. But the time for change is now. And we, as optimists, will take inspiration from these 'makers of modern Dalit history'.

Notes

1. Raj Kumar, *Dalit Literature and Criticism*, Orient BlackSwan, 2019, p. 7.

2. Salim Yusufji, *Ambedkar: The Attendant Details*, Navayana, 2017, p. 108.

3. Manoranjan Byapari, *Interrogating My Chandal Life: An Autobiography of a Dalit*, Sage Publications, 2018.

4. Kumar, *Dalit Literature and Criticism*, p. 11.

5. Ibid., p. 47.

6. Id., p. 54.

7. Arjun Dangle, *Poisoned Bread: Translations from Modern Marathi Dalit Literature*, Orient BlackSwan, 1992.

8. This resolution was published in vol. 4, no. 3 of *Prabuddha Bharat* in 1958 (Dangle 242).

9. Urmila Pawar and Meenakshi Moon, *We Also Made History: Women in the Ambedkarite Movement*, translated from Marathi (2006) and with an introduction by Wandana Sonalkar, Zubaan Books, 2008, Chapter 9.

10. Joshil K. Abraham and Judith Misrahi-Barak, eds, *Dalit Literatures in India*, Second edition, Routeledge India, 2018, p. 201.

11. Ibid., pp. 302–04. Jadhav's book was later published as *Untouchable: My Family's Triumphant Journey Out of the Caste-System in Modern India* for wider circulation.

12. Kumar, *Dalit Literature and Criticism*, p. 116.

13. Ibid.

14. Mohan Das Namishray, *Dalit Freedom Fighters*, Gyan Publishing House, 2009, p. 30.

15. Yuval Noah Harari, *Homo Deus: A Brief History of Tomorrow*, Vintage, 2017.

16. Kumar, *Dalit Literature and Criticism*, p. 4.

17. Ibid., p. 5.

18. Id., p. 11.

19. Release of Primary Census Abstract Data Highlights, Census of India 2011, 30 April 2013, http://idsn.org/wp-content/uploads/user_folder/pdf/New_files/India/2013/INDIA_CENSUS_ABSTRACT-2011-Data_on_SC-STs.pdf (accessed on 30 January 2020)

20. B.R. Ambedkar, *Three Historical Addresses of Dr. Babasaheb Ambedkar in the Constituent Assembly: In Search of Remedies for Current Instability of Polity*, Dr Ambedkar Foundation Research Cell, 1999.

21. Balachandra Mungekar, *The Essential Ambedkar*, Rupa Publications, 2017, p. 317.

22. 'I have a Dream by Martin Luther King, Jr; August 28, 1963', The Avalon Project: Documents in Law, History and Diplomacy, Yale Law School, https://avalon.law.yale.edu/20th_century/mlk01.asp (accessed on 30 January 2020).

23. Constitutional Provision, Article 39, Certain principles of policy to be followed by the State, Ministry of Human Resource Development, Government of India, https://mhrd.gov.in/directive_principles_of_state_policy_article-39 (accessed on 30 January 2020).

24. 'PM Inaugurates Indira Gandhi Conference: "An Indian Social Democracy: from Political Vision to Practical Possibility"', Prime Minister's Office, 19 November 2010, http://pib.nic.in/newsite/erelcontent.aspx?relid=67329 (accessed on 18 July 2018).

25. Ravindra Kumar, 'Gandhi: Democracy and Fundamental Rights', Extracts of Lecture at the Centre for Civil Society, University of Kwazulu-Natal, S. A., http://ccs.ukzn.ac.za/files/Gandhi%20Democracy%20and%20Fundamental%20Rights.pdf (accessed on 19 July 2018); Ravindra Kumar and Kiran Lata Dangwal, 'Gandhi: Democracy and Fundamental Rights', Gandhi Research Foundation, https://www.mkgandhi.org/articles/democracy.htm (accessed on 19 July 2018).

26. Rai Sengupta, '2017 Timeline of Atrocities Against Dalits: UP, Rajasthan Top The List', Citizen, 29 November 2017, https://www.thecitizen.in/index.php/en/newsdetail/index/2/12381/2017-timeline-of-atrocities-against-dalits-up-rajasthan-top-the-list (accessed on 30 January 2020).

27. Narayan Aditi, Facebook profile, https://www.facebook.com/aditi.narayani?fref=search (accessed on 15 February 2019).

28. Amit Thorat and Omkar Joshi, 'So Who Is Practicing Untouchability in India?', India Human Development Survey, 26 August 2016, https://www.ihds.umd.edu/blog/so-who-practicing-untouchability-india (accessed on 30 January 2020).

29. Shalini Nair, 'Centre offers 2.5 lakh for every inter-caste marriage with a Dalit', https://indianexpress.com/article/india/centre-offers-rs-2-5-lakh-for-every-inter-caste-marriage-with-a-dalit-4969989/.

30. Diane Coffey, Payal Hathi, Nidhi Khurana and Amit Thorat, 'Explicit Prejudice', *Economic & Political Weekly*, vol. 53, no. 1, 6 January 2018, pp. 46–54.

31. Pankaj Madan and Mark Alexander Friedrich, 'Attitudes, Anxieties and Aspirations of India's Youth: Changing Patterns', Centre for the Study of Developing Societies (CSDS) and Konrad- Adenauer-Stiftung, 4 April 2017, https://www.kas.de/en/web/indien/veranstaltungsberichte/detail/-/content/einstellungen-sorgen-und-ambitionen-von-indiens-jugend-sich-veraendernde-muster1 (accessed on 6 July 2018).

32. Paul Attewell and Sukhadeo Thorat, 'The Legacy of Social Exclusion', *Economic & Political Weekly*, vol. 42, no. 41, 13 October 2007, pp. 41–45.

33. Ajit Kumar Jha, 'The Dalits | Still untouchable', *India Today*, 3 February 2016, https://www.indiatoday.in/magazine/the-big-story/story/20160215-dalits-untouchable-rohith-vemula-caste-discrimination-828418-2016-02-03 (accessed on 30 January 2020).

34. Alison Saldanha and Chaitanya Mallapur, 'Over Decade, Crime Rate Against Dalits Up 25%, Cases Pending Investigation Up 99%', IndiaSpend, 4 April 2018, https://www.indiaspend.com/over-a-decade-crime-rate-against-dalits-rose-by-746-746/ (last accessed on 24 January 2020).

35. Sarah Hafeez, 'Kasganj: Finally, UP Dalit groom allowed to take wedding procession through Thakur-dominated village', *The Indian Express*, 9 April 2018, http://indianexpress.com/article/india/kasganj-dalit-groom-wedding-baraat-thakur-jatav-uttar-pradesh-caste-5129742/ (accessed on 10 July 2018).

36. 'Gujarat: 21-Year-Old Dalit Youth Killed Allegedly For Owning, Riding Horse', *Outlook*, 31 March 2018, https:// www.outlookindia.com/website/ story/in- gujarat-21-year- old-dalit-youth- killed-allegedly- for-riding-horse/ 310251 (accessed on 6 July 2018).

37. Bhasker Tripathi and Shreya Khaitan, 'Dalit Bridegrooms On Horses Challenge India's Caste Status Quo', IndiaSpend, 27 April 2018, https://www.indiaspend.com/dalit-bridegrooms-on-horses-

challenge-indias-caste-status-quo-97061/ (accessed on 30 January 2020).

38. Jaya Menon, 'Dalit Woman Panchayat President Auctioned for 2.16 Lakh in TN Village', *Indian Express*, 19 November 2006, http://archive.indianexpress.com/news/dalit-woman-panchayat-president-auctioned-for--2.16-lakh-in-tn-village/16909/ (accessed on 6 July 2018).

39. Kenneth J. Cooper, 'India's Majority Lower Castes Are Minor Voice in Newspapers', *Washington Post*, 5 September 1996, https://www.washingtonpost.com/archive/politics/1996/09/05/indias-majority-lower-castes-are-minor-voice-in-newspapers/4acb79e3-13d6-4084-b1d9-b09c6ed4f963/ (accessed on 6 July 2018).

40. B.N. Uniyal, 'In Search of a Dalit Journalist', *Pioneer*, 16 November 1996.

41. Ojha Jai Prakash, *DNA of Dalit Movement*, Partridge Publishing, 2014.

42. Harry Stevens, 'Seven decades after independence, most Dalit farmers still landless', *Hindustan Times*, 13 February 2018, https://www.hindustantimes.com/interactives/dalit-farmers-landless-agricultural-labourers-minimum-support-price/ (accessed on 30 January 2020).

43. Suraj Yengde, 'To make their voices heard, Dalits need to protest 365 days a year', *Hindustan Times*, 12 April 2018, https://www.hindustantimes.com/analysis/to-make-their-voices-heard-dalits-need-to-protest-365-days-a-year/story-NzBRrcl04igToiL51UlKQL.html (accessed on 6 July 2018).

44. Venkatesh Athreya R. Chandra, 'Dalits and Land Issues', *Frontline*, vol. 17, no. 12, 10 June 2000.

45. P.S. Krishnan, 'Importance of giving land to Dalits', *Frontline*, 13 September 2019.

46. Ibid.

47. Ram Madhav, 'What Dalits Want', *Indian Express*, 13 April 2016, https://indianexpress.com/article/opinion/columns/ambedkar-dalit-status-equality-justice-discrimination-what-dalits-want/ (accessed on 6 July 2018).

48. Mohan Dass Namishray, 'Dalits and Memories of 1857', *Dalit Freedom Fighters*, Gyan Publishing House, 2009.

49. Ibid., p. 22.

50. Roger Boesche, *Kautilya: The First Great Political Realist*, HarperCollins, 2017.

51. Vivek Kumar, *India's Roaring Revolution: Dalit Assertion and New Horizons*, Gagan Deep Publications, 2006.

52. Table 1.2.14, Literacy Rate for Scheduled Castes (SCs) and Total Population in India Time Series Data–1961 to 2011. Handbook on Social Welfare Statistics, Ministry of Social Justice & Empowerment Department of Social Justice & Empowerment Statistics Division New Delhi, Government of India, January 2016), p. 42.

53. 'Text of PMs Speech at Ramanujacharya Stamp Release Event', Press Information Bureau, Government of India, Prime Minister's Office, 1 May 2017, http://pib.nic.in/newsite/PrintRelease. aspx?relid=161430 (accessed on 26 January 2020).

54. B.R. Ambedkar, *The Untouchables: Who Were They and Why They Became Untouchables*, Kalpaz Publications, 2017.

55. Liz Mathew, 'Presidential Polls: The Dalit Push', *Indian Express*, 25 June 2017, https://indianexpress.com/article/india/presidential-polls-dalit-ram-nath-kovind-meira-kumar-bjp-opposition-4720479/ (accessed on 6 July 2018).

56. https://www.standupmitra.in/.

57. Werner Sollors, Caldwell Titcomb, Thomas A. Underwood and Randall Kennedy, *Blacks at Harvard: A Documentary History of African-American Experience at Harvard and Radcliffe*, NYU Press, 1993, p. 365.

58. Karl R. Popper, E. H. Gombrich and Alan Ryan, *The Open Society and Its Enemies: New One-Volume Edition*, Princeton University Press, 2013.

Ayyankali

The advent of the nineteenth century saw many social reformers playing pivotal roles in the cause of Dalit dignity. Some of the key causes they fought for were issues of education and representation, which they believed would instil faith in the hearts of the downtrodden Dalits. These great visionaries worked untiringly towards the empowerment of the lower castes, in particular those considered to be 'outcastes'.

One such visionary was Ayyankali, a subaltern hero from Kerala. Ayyankali, born on 28 August 1863, was the oldest of eight[1] children born to Ayyan and Mala, who were part of the Pulayar community, considered 'rural slaves' in Kerala. Venganoor, the village from which Ayyankali hailed, is said to have seen deep-rooted social divisions.[2] Robin Jeffrey, a Canadian professor who specializes in research on Kerala, in his book *The Decline of Nair Dominance*,[3] has detailed how people from the community of Pulayars, even if allowed to meet anyone from another community, were not allowed to touch or eat with them.

Travancore (now a part of modern-day Kerala) where Ayyankali was born meted out despicable treatment to the untouchables. The word pulaya was derived from the word pula (pollution), they were not allowed to use the word 'I' but only adiyan (your slave)[4]. Ayyankali's father, Ayyan, worked as an adiyan of Panangott Ottilathu Parameswaran Pillai.[5]

Although the Government of India, under Prime Minister Narendra Modi, did observe and celebrate the birth anniversary of Ayyankali in 2014, and previously Indira Gandhi unveiled a statue of the social reformer in the 1980 at Thiruvananthapuram,[6] Ayyankali remains a neglected figure in the annals of history, so much so that some historians have written that some of his own family members did not follow him after his death.[7] Ayyankali rose to prominence as the key Dalit voice in the social milieu of Kerala of the time, when Dalits were derided not only as untouchables but 'unseeables' and 'unapproachables' as well.

Ayyankali was a rebel with a cause. One of his first acts of assertion was at the age of seven. He retaliated and hit an upper caste boy for hitting him first.[8]

Even as he stood firm in his commitment that Dalits should have their share of representation and asserted this, he did play the role of disruptor but did not go against the state—and in this lay Ayyankali's greatness and strength. He initiated revolutionary steps, such as the use of folk music to register a strong protest against the discrimination faced by his community. The performers dressed as people from other communities, such as the Nairs, to defy prevalent social conventions. Ayyankali fearlessly and freely travelled by *villuvandi* (bullock cart) on roads that were restricted to use by upper castes or members of other communities only. He also enabled access to education for children belonging to his community and vociferously campaigned against the traditional stricture that prohibited female members of the Pulayar community from clothing their upper body when in public. These efforts sowed the seeds of a future Dalit-led empowerment. He was never a proponent of hate or vitriol against the system and found a way within it to envision new measures.

Ayyankali foreshadowed much of what B.R. Ambedkar would later go on to propagate—representation, inclusion of the downtrodden segments of society into the mainstream, reaffirmation of the importance of education and the principle of gender justice. These have all been strongly embedded in the Constitution of India in the twentieth century. Unfortunately, Ayyankali's words were rarely read, practised, reported or acknowledged, for some may have wanted to avoid an uprising while others were simply apathetic. Rarely does one see mainstream authors, academics or the media reporting on Ayyankali's accomplishments for the Dalits. Several key social reformers and integrators who should have be celebrated and honoured have instead been forgotten. In fact, Indians today should proclaim with pride that several human rights movements have their roots in the words of social activists such as Ayyankali.

To understand the significance of his contribution, it is vital that one understands the circumstances under which Ayyankali fought for the rights of the oppressed.

India in the nineteenth century suffered from rampant caste discrimination. Y.B. Satyanarayana wrote of deep-rooted caste divisions in rural India in his book *My Father Baliah*.[9] He writes that in a residential colony, the houses of the upper castes came first, followed by those of the lower castes. The placement of the houses were such that the wind blew from the houses of the upper castes to those of the lower castes, as the opposite would be inauspicious.

Such discrimination also existed in Kerala, where Dalits, it was said, were expected to maintain a physical distance of at least sixty-four steps from the Nairs and 128 steps from the Namboodiris, both upper castes.[10] The Pulayar caste, to which Ayyankali belonged, was not permitted to buy bullocks or carts, or walk on roads reserved for the upper castes. But he defied these norms and walked on public roads alongside a bullock cart bought with his own money. With this notable act, by doing the unthinkable,

Ayyankali succeeded in subverting the traditional order. Under Ayyankali's leadership, the Dalit men fearlessly ventured into roads and marketplaces that were forbidden to the Dalits. On one occasion they were confronted by upper caste men and things turned violent, this was commonly referred to as Chaliyar riots.[11]

Dalit families in Kerala remained silent about the harassment they faced at the hands of upper castes. For example, Dalit women did not dare to speak of their sexual harassment by upper-caste men for fear of being flogged or killed. Ayyankali took matters into his own hands and created a gathering of people, comprising his young friends from the Pulayar community, who would come together to give voice to their frustration and disgust through folk dance and music at the end of each day. The efforts were slow and nascent but still gave their dissent a steady start. He devised a creative wave of rebellion and soon came to be known as 'Urpillai' (loved one) and 'Moothapillai'(elder one).[12]

Ayyankali was deeply influenced by Swami Sadananda, a reformist Nair ascetic who stood against discriminatory practices, and in this he mirrored his contemporary Narayana Guru. In 1907, Ayyankali established the Sadhu Jana Paripalana Sangham (SJPS). This institution was formed to unite members of the depressed communities beyond the traditional strongholds of the caste system. Ayyankali made the men and women remit a membership fee to be part of the Sangam.[13] It also encouraged Dalit women to play an integral role in society, which led many Dalit women to raise considerable funds for the SJPS with the slogan 'Progress through education and organization'.[14] Ayyankali was instrumental in establishing Samudhaya Kodathi[15] (community courts), whose local offices functioned in every branch of the SJPS. Some of the appeals of the lower courts were directed to the community courts of Venganur, where Ayyankali was the judge in one. These courts[16]—which had all the paraphernalia of regular courts—came into being as the regular courts did not prove effective when it came to serving the cause of the downtrodden communities. However, even as a judge, Ayyankali was more of a social reformer. He and his community had been deprived of formal education, which was why he wanted the next generation to attain the benefits of education. In 1904, Ayyankali launched a movement for Dalit education. He opened a school for Pulayar and other Dalit children at Venganoor the same year.[17]

In 1912, he was nominated to the Sree Moolam Popular Assembly by the then dewan (the equivalent of a prime minister) P. Rajagopalachari of Travancore, who noticed his reform movements and leadership skills. He was the first Dalit Pulayar to be nominated to the Assembly. This was an assembly of the representatives of the landholders and merchants in the country established by then Travancore's Dewan V.P. Madhava Rao.

Just like Nelson Mandela, who said, 'Education is a powerful tool in the world, which you can use to change the world,'[18] Ayyankali was of the view that education, and education alone, was the way forward for the empowerment of the Dalit community. He believed that modern education was the passport that would guarantee an entry into the public sphere, and that it was a powerful weapon against prejudice. It was in this context that, in 1912, he prompted the Sree Moolam Popular Assembly to issue an order mandating the admission of Dalit children into public schools. This saw great resistance from upper-caste officials in the assembly , but Ayyankali was not one to give up after coming this far. Following a struggle of almost two years, the order was finally passed in favour of Dalits by the then Travancore government in concurrence with the assembly in 1914. In fact, in one of his meetings with Mahatma Gandhi, Ayyankali affirmed that one of his earnest wishes was to see ten BA graduates from his community.[19]

Ayyankali also worked to see that Dalits were represented in the political sphere. P.K. Govinda Pillai was nominated to the Sree Moolam Popular Assembly as a representative of the SJPS by the then Dewan Rajagopalachari. Subsequently, Ayyankali was nominated to the Sree Moolam Popular Assembly on 5 December 1911. He remained a member of the assembly for twenty-two years, from 1912 to 1934. In what was another instance of his assertion, on 27 February 1912, Ayyankali came to the assembly in a bullock cart. Ayyankali, in his speeches, reiterated the importance of including at least five members of the Pulayar community into it. However, even today, a hundred years after Ayyankali's struggles, there is still inadequate representation of Dalits in the political realm.

Ayyankali, a pragmatic philosopher and guide, listed out five pillars of success that he believed were markers of progress for subaltern communities—faith in God, modern dressing, cleanliness, obedience and discipline. In the book *Ayyankali: A Dalit Leader of Organic Protest*, Meena Kandasamy and M. Nisar write that Ayyankali also began to work with the Arya Samaj, the Hindu Mahasabha, the Kerala Hindu Mission and other social reform groups to achieve his objective of integrating the subaltern community into the mainstream.

In 1888, Ayyankali was married to Chellama, with whom he had seven children. Ayyankali breathed his last on 18 June 1941. In the Indian Dalit movement, Ayyankali's momentous contribution remains a turning point in history. He encouraged the intellectual capabilities of the Dalit community and their role as citizens of India. It is civil society that shapes the actions of a country's policymakers, and the onus of bringing about transformation in society, therefore, lies with every Indian. Taking inspiration from the life and work of Ayyankali, India can strive, with such pure intention as his, to ensure that affirmative action upholds Dalit dignity.

It is no wonder that it is in Kerala, the land of social reformers and stalwarts such as Narayana Guru and Ayyankali, that the first legislation of social transformation was recently initiated. With the government-sanctioned appointment of non-Brahmin priests in state-owned temples, Kerala has given an impetus to the Dalit movement. With Dalits now performing rituals at temples, social barriers are gradually being eroded. In the times to come, we are certain to witness the upward journey of our nation as society gradually evolves.

Dalit issues ranging from justice against atrocities to representation and empowerment in society have had a predominant influence on the political narratives of India. It is imperative to see that the problem of caste is more social than political. It is often observed that social issues are turned into misguided missiles under the influence of passionate rhetoric and emotional platitudes. But ignoring the positive side of the rise of Dalits through merit alone would be a great disservice to the strength and cause of Dalit dignity.

Notes

1. S. Ambili, 'Ayyankali: A Biographical Sketch', http://kingsuniversityusa. org/pdf/article.pdf.

2. M. Nisar and Meena Kandasamy, *Ayyankali: Dalit Leader of Organic Protest*, Other Books, 2007.

3. Robin Jeffrey, *The Decline of Nair Dominance: Society and Politics in Travancore 1847–1908*, Sussex University Press, 1976.

4. Manu S. Pillai, 'The Leader on a Bullock Cart', Livemint, 14 April 2018, https://www.livemint.com/Leisure/2FuihtKsvuKWylpvtaJD7K/ The-leader-on-a-bullock-cart.html (accessed 21 March 2020).

5. Nisar and Kandasamy, *Ayyankali*, p. 68.

6. Rajesh Komath, 'Ambedkar Will Teach the Nation from His Statues', *Economic & Political Weekly*, vol. 52, nos 25–26, 29 June 2017 (accessed 7 February 2020).

7. Pillai, 'The Leader on a Bullock Cart'.

8. Dr S. Ambili, 'Ayyankali: A Biographical Sketch', http:// kingsuniversityusa.org/pdf/article.pdf (accessed on 7 February 2020).

9. Y.B. Satyanarayana, *My Father Baliah*, HarperCollins, 2011.

10. As per the authors' conversation with Prof. Vivek Kumar, Professor, JNU undertaken as part of research for the book.

11. Nisar and Kandasamy, *Ayyankali*, p. 70.
12. Omprakash Kashyap, 'Saint Ayyankali: The harbinger of a social revolution', Forward Press, 18 July 2019.
13. Nisar and Kandasamy, *Ayyankali*, p. 76.
14. Poulasta Chakraborthy, 'Mahatma Ayyankali – A Brief Profile', India Facts, 12 September 2014, http://indiafacts.org/mahatma-ayyankali-brief-profile/ (accessed on 26 January 2020).
15. S. Prathika, 'Sadhu Jana Paripala Sangam', *Research Journal of Indian Studies* (accessed on 7 February 2020).
16. Ibid.
17. Omprakash Kashyap, 'Saint Ayyankali: The harbinger of a social revolution', Forward Press, 18 July 2019.
18. Nelson Mandela, 'Lighting your way to a better future', paper presented at the launch of Mindset Network, Johannesburg, 16 July 2003, www.mandela.gov.za/mandela_speeches/2003/030716_mindset.htm (accessed on 18 July 2018).
19. 'Ayyankali: A Brief Biography of a Dalit Freedom Fighter', https://www.facebook.com/notes/gowthama-meena/ayyan-kali-a-brief-biography-of-a-dalit-freedom-fighter/447633028643783/ (accessed on 31 March 2020).

Babu Jagjivan Ram

In many parts of India today, Dalits still have to take their dead to separate graveyards or crematoriums; upper castes still serve them food and beverages in separate utensils; and there are stories of how priests leave the temple before young Dalit couples can arrive there to be wedded, so they don't have to open the temple gates for them. The Temple-Entry Movement of the late nineteenth and early twentieth centuries required the upper castes to allow the entry of all communities, including Dalits. Given that Dalits still have to go through such discrimination today, it is not hard to imagine what things would have been like in the 1990s.

Much of Babu Jagjivan Ram's life, who was born on 5 April 1908 in Chandwa vilage, Bihar, was spent ensuring that Dalits got respect within the Hindu fold. Fondly known as Babuji, he was of the firm belief that casteism was a rot in Indian society that could only be fought by reforming the Hindu faith and changing social attitudes.[1]

Babuji was only six and had only just begun school when he lost his father Shobhi Ram. The young boy was left in the care of his mother Vasanti Devi. However, despite social and economic hardships, she insisted that her son continue his education. The Chamar community, which Babuji belonged to, were those who were assigned the work of removing dead animals from the vicinity and making leather from their skin; they also undertook scavenging work. The community was denied all right to property.

When Babuji topped his class in Standard X and did not have the money to continue his studies, local nuns offered him free education at their Lucknow-based Christian school. They also promised to send him to the US for higher studies. However, Babuji's mother politely refused the offer, as she did not want to send her son to a Christian school or have him converted to Christianity.[2]

Babuji joined the Town School in Arrah in 1922. His school days were full of blatant and constant caste discrimination. It is possible that these events impacted his young mind in a deep way. Dalit students were given a separate water pitcher to drink water from, and upper-caste boys would refuse to drink from the earthen pitcher that a young Babuji might have accidentally touched. One day, an outraged Babuji refused to tolerate this insult any longer and broke the pitcher in protest. When it was replaced, he broke it again. This led to a common water pitcher being installed for all the students of the school.[3] Despite the ignominious caste discrimination he faced, he passed his exams with first-division marks, even achieving full marks in sanskrit and mathematics. By the time he completed high school, he had earned the reputation of being a cut above the rest.

He walked three kilometres early in the morning every day to the Arrah railway station to read *The Statesman* newspaper to keep abreast of national and international developments. He discovered Bankimchandra Chattopadhyay's *Anandmath*,[4] a book popular among revolutionaries during the Indian freedom movement. He was so inspired by it that he learnt Bengali just to read the book. As a voracious reader in his university days later in Kolkata (then Calcutta), Babuji would spend an hour in the library every day. He was fluent in Hindi, English, Bengali and Sanskrit, in addition to his native Bhojpuri.

His father, Shobhi Ram, was a farmer and a mahant of the Shivnarayani sect, a local cultural and religious group. Inspired by his father's involvement in religious and cultural activities and having understood the importance of the following that Guru Ravidas had among the Dalits, especially the Chamars, Babuji established the Akhil Bharatiya Ravidas Mahasabha (ABRM) in Calcutta (present-day Kolkata). He went on to organize a number of Ravidas *sammelan*s to celebrate Guru Ravidas Jayanti (or the birth anniversary of Guru Ravidas) in different parts of eastern India.

Even though Babuji aspired to be a scientist, his passion for serving his motherland began when he was quite young. One of his foremost initiatives was to champion the right to vote for the depressed classes. His daughter, Meira Kumar, former Speaker in the Lok Sabha, talks about his efforts in one of her speeches:

> In this connection [to ensure Dalits get the invaluable right to vote] he met Mansfield, the then Reforms Minister in Bihar. The same year he also appeared before the Hammond Commission which had come from England to examine the various issues concerning the voting rights of Dalits. He was acutely aware that without the social and political upliftment of the backward classes, our democracy would remain irrelevant to a large section of our society.[5]

One of his other significant efforts at a young age was to bring together the agricultural labour force of the Dalits in a movement, with the slogan 'Land to the actual tiller of the soil'.[6] Babuji was also well known for his relentless social work, including his relief efforts during the 1934 Nepal–Bihar earthquake. With such commitment to public life from a young age, Babuji went on to become an influential and renowned leader. When a measure of popular rule was introduced under the Government of India Act of 1935 and the Dalits were given representation in the legislatures, Babuji found himself nominated to the Bihar legislative council in 1936 at the age of twenty-eight due to his in-depth and first-hand knowledge of the sociopolitical and economical scenario in Bihar. This was the start of a remarkable political career.

In 1937, he stood as a candidate for the All India Depressed Classes League that he had founded; he was also elected unopposed to the Bihar legislative assembly from East Central Shahabad (Rural). He ensured the unopposed victory of the All India Depressed Classes League candidates in each of the fourteen reserved constituencies. With such a decisive victory, Babuji emerged as a parliamentarian of note, and this earned him an invitation to join the Congress party.

On 30 August 1946, Babuji was one of the twelve leaders of the country who were invited by the then viceroy of India, Lord Wavell, to become part of the Interim Government. He was the only representative Dalit in the Interim Government, formed on 2 September 1946, in which he held the Labour portfolio.

Babuji's contribution to the Constituent Assembly is noteworthy. He played an active role in formulating provisions that would safeguard the interests of Dalits. He also ensured that the Constitution of India had enough provisions to forbid any practice of untouchability or discrimination on the grounds of caste. The provision for state intervention for the advancement of socially backward classes by way of reservation in public employment and seats in legislatures for the scheduled castes and scheduled tribes owes its success to leaders such as Babuji. He was instrumental in the passing of the Protection of Civil Rights Act, 1955.

As former Indian president Pranab Mukherjee said, 'Babu Jagjivan Ram was a valiant fighter in India's freedom struggle and a great inspirer and organizer of people against oppression. He was a powerful orator, a distinguished parliamentarian and an able administrator.'[7]

Babuji urged the Dalits 'to struggle for a socially interdependent society which would be so changed and revolutionized that they could participate in it on terms of equality of rights and obligations'.[8] It was his life's mission to strive for the welfare of the depressed classes. In contributing to the national debate, Babuji reiterated that his fight against casteism was based on his abiding faith in the values of a democratic society and in the process of transformation through constitutionally established systems. 'Malice towards none and charity for all' was his motto, as he campaigned tirelessly to educate people so they could understand and assert their rights.

Individual freedom and human dignity were of paramount importance for him.

Babuji chose to strive for equity and social justice from within the folds of Hinduism. He was the only leader from the Congress party to be present at the meeting in which the Vishwa Hindu Parishad (VHP) was formed. He was also responsible for the Vishwanath temple in Kashi, the Meenakshi temple in Madurai and the Jagannath temple in Puri opening their doors to Dalits.

His Calcutta University days are also marked with some remarkable achievements. In fact, a phrase, '*Tui shobjaanta* Jagjivan Ram*', which means 'you know-it-all Jagjivan Ram', has made its way into Bengali parlance, showing the extent of his popularity even in Calcutta.

But what made leaders such as Netaji Subhas Chandra Bose take notice of him was the *mazdoor* rally he organized at Wellington Square, which was attended by more than 35,000 people.[9]

One of the most striking incidents of Babuji's life was one that brought him face to face with death. In the words of his daughter, Meira Kumar, this is what happened:

It was rainy season and the tiny rivulet Gangi, which crisscrossed the eastern side of our village, had swelled. One hot afternoon Babuji and his friend went for a swim after school. The current was too powerful for the young swimmers. Being closer to the shore, the friend managed to come out; Babuji could not. Overcome by fierce mid-stream current he was fast drifting away when a woman spotted him. She had a long stick for driving her pigs. She rushed and extended the stick to rescue him. He saw the stick, outstretched his arm, held it tight and using all his might came out. It all happened in a flash, but it kindled a light within him forever.[10]

She says that the incident became a turning point in his life, one to which he would turn to again and again for sustenance, especially in trying moments in his efforts to bring about social change as also in his own life's philosophy.

Babuji served the Parliament for an uninterrupted fifty years, from 1936 to 1986.[11] He also remained a minister for thirty years in various Congress governments. As labour minister (two stints, 1946–50 and 1966–67), during his first tenure, he laid the foundation for a new era of labour welfare and industrial productivity in the form of the Minimum Wages Act 1948 and Employees' Provident Funds and Miscellaneous Provisions Act 1952. As railway minister (1957–62), he gave a new thrust to the modernization of the railways. As agricultural minister (1967–70), he helped the country recover from the clutches of a severe drought and heralded the Green Revolution, along with helping establish krishi vigyan kendras, or agricultural extension centres, to help farmers forge an understanding between their field expereinces and latest research expertise.[12] As defence minister, under the leadership of then prime minister Indira Gandhi, he oversaw the liberation of Bangladesh. In *The Blood Telegram*,[13] Gary J. Bass's work on the liberation war of Bangladesh, he called Babu Jagjivan Ram the most 'hawkish' defence minister, owing to his role in the victory of India in the war of 1971. In this war, which played a pivotal role in shaping the history of South Asia, Babuji not only motivated the Indian armed forces to fight for the liberation of another country, but also kept his promise to the people that the war would not be fought on Indian soil.

Babuji was also responsible for cultivating leadership among the Dalits. His efforts through the Congress for Democracy party, which he formed in 1977, led to the swearing in of Damodaram Sanjivayya and Bhola Paswan Shastri as chief ministers of Andhra Pradesh and Bihar, respectively.

When Babuji breathed his last on 6 July 1986, he had become a role model for many in the public sphere. As a powerful symbol of social change, Babuji's life can be a source of inspiration for today's citizens. He was a social worker, a grass-roots leader with a nuanced understanding of social structure, an erudite parliamentarian, an able administrator, a leader of the depressed classes and the Dalits, and a cabinet minister.

In June 1935, Babuji was married to Indrani Devi, with whom he had two children, Suresh and Meira Kumar.

On Babuji's 108th birth anniversary, the Government of India launched the 'Stand Up India' scheme to support entrepreneurship among women and the scheduled castes and scheduled tribes. Organizations such as DICCI are even today working tirelessly for the emancipation of Dalits through economic empowerment. As Babuji said, 'In the progress of the country lies our progress; in its salvation our salvation, and in its emancipation, our emancipation.'[14] In this, Babuji today stands as not just a personality but an idea that has shaped the empowerment of Dalits in India.

Notes

1. Sanjay Paswan, 'Remembering Babuji', *Indian Express*. https://indianexpress.com/article/opinion/columns/babu-jagjivan-ram-dali-leader-babuji-2902184/

2. Tarun Vijay, 'Why no Bharat Ratna for Babu Jagjivan Ram?', *Times of India*, 3 July 2016, https://timesofindia.indiatimes.com/blogs/indus-calling/why-no-bharat-ratna-for-babu-jagjivan-ram-is-it-

because-he-was-rebel-democrat-and-faithful-hindu/ (accessed on 31 March 2020.

3. R.C. Rajamani, 'Remembering Babuji', *Hindu Business Line*, 4 April 2013. https://www.thehindubusinessline.com/opinion/columns/Remembering-Babuji/article20598620.ece.

4. Bankimchandra Chattopadhyay, *Anandmath*, Diamond Books, 2012.

5. Address by former Lok Sabha Speaker, Meira Kumar, as part of the fourth Babu Jagjivan Ram Memorial Lecture held on 6 April 2011, http://164.100.47.194/loksabha/writereaddata//JPI/JPI_Sep_2011.pdf (accessed on 27 January 2020).

6. Sanjay Paswan and Pramanshi Jaideva, eds, *Encyclopaedia of Dalits in India: Vol. 4*, Kalpaz Publications, 2002, p. 83.

7. Jagjivan Ram, *Babu Jagjivan Ram in Parliament: A Commemorative Volume*, Lok Sabha Secretariat, 2005.

8. Former vice president Hamid Ansari's speech as part of the Babu Jagjivan Memorial Lecture, 'Vice President Delivers Babu Jagjivan Ram Memorial Lecture', 6 April 2011, http://pib.nic.in/newsite/PrintRelease.aspx?relid=71509 (accessed on 28 January 2020).

9. 'Jagjivan Ram an Example of Development Politics', *Hindu*, 28 September 2016, https://www.thehindu.com/todays-paper/tp-national/tp-newdelhi/per cent60Jagjivan-Ram-an-example-of-development-politics/article14745585.ece (accessed on 10 July 2018).

10. 'Empowerment of the Scheduled Cast Community: Contribution of BabuJagjivan Ram', India Latest News, 13 February 2017, https://www.indialatestnews.com/2017/02/empowerment-of-scheduled-cast-community.html

11. 'Tributes paid to Babu Jagjivan Ram on his 104th birth anniversary', *Times of India*, 5 April 2011, http://timesofindia.indiatimes.com/articleshow/7873307.cms?utm_source=contentofinterest&utm_medium=text&utm_campaign=cppst (accessed on 31 March 2020).

12. Former vice president Hamid Ansari's speech as part of Babu Jagjivan Memorial Lecture, 'Vice President Delivers Babu Jagjivan Ram Memorial Lecture', 5 April 2011, http://pib.nic.in/newsite/PrintRelease.aspx?relid=71509.

13. Gary J. Bass, *The Blood Telegram: Nixon, Kissinger, and a Forgotten Genocide*, Vintage, reprint edition, 2014.

14. Paswan and Jaideva, *Encyclopaedia of Dalits in India*,vol. 4, p. 118.

Dakshayani Velayudhan

On 29 May 1917, a social reformer named Sahodaran Ayyappan made a powerful statement against the caste system prevalent in Kerala by bringing together various castes, including his own Ezhava community, for an inter-caste *panthibhojanam* (community feast) at Thundidaparambu, Chirayi. T. Bhaskaran describes this momentous event in his book *Maharishi Sree Narayana Guru*, in which he also mentions the role played by a community member named Ayyar and his son:

> In the *Panthibhojanam*, rice along with a side dish made of jackfruit seeds and chickpeas were served. A Pulayar (a Dalit caste) named Ayyar who is from Pallipuram served the food. He was already scheduled to do so. Ayyar had come along with his son. But since the number of people participating had grown much beyond what they expected, everyone got a small amount of food. In the middle of the crowd, Ayyar's son was made to sit. When the child had mixed the rice and the curry, everyone tasted a mouthful from his plate, and that was the famous '*Misrabhojanam*' (also called *Panthibhojanam*).[1]

The reason for a strong statement against the caste system was the miserable state of the Pulayars, the Dalit community from which Dakshayani Velayudhan came from. They had to face the brunt of the upper caste in pursuit of social cohesion and dignity.In those days, social divisions, and hence social inequality, was more entrenched. Members of the Dalit communities in Kerala were not allowed to walk on the same roads as members of the upper caste, nor were they permitted to be 'seen' by them. But reformers such as Dakshayani Velayudhan, India's first Dalit woman Constituent Assembly member, ensured the empowerment of the downtrodden, especially the Dalits, through representation and not just mere symbolism.

Velayudhan, although instrumental in the drafting of the Constitution, has largely remained on the fringes of the academic and thought-leadership circles in India. Born on 4 July 1912 in Mulavukad, a small island off the coast of Cochin (now Kochi), Velayudhan's life and politics were shaped by the rigid caste system of Kerala. She belonged to the Pulaya community, considered to be the earliest inhabitants of the state but subjected to acute discrimination by the upper castes.

The Pulayas were mainly agricultural labourers and were prohibited from walking on public roads or drawing water from public wells. Pulaya women were only permitted to wear bead necklaces to cover their breasts. According to *A Report on Slavery* by an Indian law commissioner in 1841,[2] societal restrictions imposed on this community were so stringent that when members went out, they had to make others aware of their presence by loudly uttering certain words every four or five steps they took. Pulayas had to adhere to the demands of the upper caste by working under them at all times.

K.P. Karuppan, who fought for the rights of the Pulayas, wrote in a report in 1934 about the conditions of the community at the beginning of the twentieth century: 'I saw them only in a dirty mundu (a garment worn around the waist). The women were all half-naked. Some of them covered themselves with grass.'[3] The Pulayas could not even cut their hair or have their children enrol in government schools. Apart from not having access to public roads and markets in mainland Ernakulam, they couldn't even enter hospitals.

Despite having to face discrimination at every step while growing up, Dakshayani never gave up on her goal of educating herself. Incidentally, in those days in Ernakulam, children from scheduled caste communities could be admitted into certain schools for free. Dakshayani grabbed this opportunity. She studied in St Mary's school Mulavukad and MLC School, Chathyathu. There were hardships, of course, but it not deter her from getting a bachelor's degree and subsequently completing a teacher's training course from the Madras University. Her studies were supported by scholarships from the state government of Cochin. From 1935 to 1945, she worked as a teacher at the government high schools in Trichur and Tripunithura.[4]

Swami Vivekananda rightly said, 'A few sincere, wholehearted, energetic men and women can do more in a year than a mob can in a century.'[5] Dakshayani, which means Durga and one fiercely independent in thought and opinion, went on to be the first Dalit girl to wear a piece of clothing on her upper body in Kerala, and also the first female Dalit graduate in India. Signs of social change was discernible even in her name, as Pulayas were expected to be named only in a certain way.[6] Naming her 'Dakshayani' was a departure from norm, because it was similar to those one would find in the Ezhava community, which, while also being a backward community, was considered above the Pulayas. Dakshayani wrote that such a name was 'never used by the depressed classes. Pulaya women said that I am given the name of an Ezhava (backward caste) girl. Pulayas had peculiar names like Azhaki, Poomala, Chakki, Kali, Kurumba, Thara, Kilipakka, etc.'[7]

The situation of Dalit women in India needs special attention. When Mayawati was elected the chief minister of Uttar Pradesh, former prime minister P.V. Narasimha Rao called it 'a miracle of democracy'.[8] Dalit women are one of the largest socially segregated groups in the world and make up 2 per cent of the world's total population. They are discriminated against three times over—they are poor, they are women and they are Dalit. They are half the overall Dalit population and close to 16.3 per cent of the total Indian female population.[9]

It is in this context that one must understand the prevalent circumstances under which Dakshayani lived. Despite the constant battle against social injustice, at one point in her life, she could no longer bear the enormous social stigma and institutional discrimination she faced as an educator, and decided to pursue politics. She felt that this would help her get justice for her community and also serve her country at the same time. Dakshayani, who followed in the footsteps of her brother K.P. Vallon, was nominated to the Cochin legislative council in 1945. On 2 August 1945, Dakshayani spoke for the first time in the council, and in English. In 1946, she was nominated to the Constituent Assembly from the Madras presidency. In that congregation of 389 people in the Constituent Assembly, there were just fifteen women—and thirty-four-year-old Dakshayani Velayudhan was one of them.

In her blog Women Architects of the Indian Republic,[10] Priya Ravichandran details the objectives with which Dakshayani functioned in the Constituent Assembly:

Dakshayani's term in the constituent assembly was defined by two objectives, both inspired and moulded by her time with Gandhi and Ambedkar. One was to make the assembly go beyond framing a constitution and to give people 'a new framework of life' and two, to use the opportunity to make untouchability illegal, unlawful and ensure a 'moral safeguard that gives real protection to the underdogs' in India. Her idea of moral safeguards rested on the idea that an independent

India as a 'socialist republic' would give equality of status and guarantee an immediate removal of social disabilities that would enable the Harijans to enjoy the same freedom that the rest of the country enjoyed.

Dakshayani's speeches in the Constituent Assembly were dismissive of separate electorates and reservations for the scheduled castes. This was in keeping with her notion that an independent India should work towards creating a stronger, common national identity rather than maintain practices that would deepen the social fissures that the British left behind.

In her words on 28 August 1947, she noted that:

As long as the Scheduled Castes or the Harijans, or by whatever name they may be called, are economic slaves of other people, there is no meaning demanding either separate electorates or joint electorates or any other kind of electorates with this kind of percentage . . . Personally speaking, I am not in favour of any kind of reservation in any place whatsoever.[11]

Dakshayani was not satisfied with the way the Constitution had been framed. In view of this, she presented the fascinating idea of putting the Constitution through a test. She suggested that the draft constitution be put to a vote during the first general elections to test its mettle with the people who would ultimately use it.

In 1940, Dakshayani married Dalit leader Raman Kelan Velayudhan, the uncle of K.R. Narayanan who would go on to become the first Dalit president of India. The wedding took place at the Gandhi ashram in Wardha, in a ceremony officiated by a leper and attended by Mahatma Gandhi and his wife Kasturba. Dakshayani later became a member of the provisional parliament, and her husband a member of Parliament in 1952, which made them the first Dalit couple in Parliament.[12] Unlike her mother and older siblings, Dakshayani did not convert to Christianity.

She remained within the ambit of Hinduism and continued her pursuit of social cohesion.

In the Constituent Assembly, she argued in favour of Article 11 of the draft constitution (Article 17 of the Constitution), which abolishes untouchability and makes it punishable by law. Her stance was: 'We cannot expect a Constitution without a clause relating to untouchability.'[13]

Today India is also party to the Convention on the Elimination of All Forms of Discrimination against Women (CEDAW). The government has an obligation to ensure that women can realize their rights. It is in this context that the government of the day has to do more than just pass legislations to protect and respect human rights. It must take all measures, including policy and budgetary ones, so that women get their rights. It also has an obligation to punish those who engage in caste-based violence and discrimination. In addition to CEDAW, India is also party to the The United Nations International Covenant of Civil and Political Rights. Based on this treaty, the Government of India has the responsibility to ensure that Dalit women have access to human rights, such as the right to life; freedom from torture or from cruel, inhuman or degrading treatment or punishment; freedom from slavery; the right to be equal before the court; the right to recognition as a person before the law; the right to privacy; the right to marry with free and full consent; and the right to take part in public affairs.[14] The life and dignity of Dalit women depend on the realization of each of these human rights.

Dakshayani passed away on 20 July 1978, having inspired thousands in the way she held her head high even in the face of adversity. Today steady strides are being made in the empowerment of Dalits and Dalit women. For instance, the National Federation of Dalit Women (NFDW), launched by Dalit women, is tasked with introducing positive changes in the lives of Dalit women, such as helping initiate legal action against caste-based atrocities, aiding their political and economic empowerment, and helping build self-confidence and leadership in them.

Many states in India are working towards putting an end to manual scavenging, which has long been solely the job of the Dalits in society. A memorandum of understanding (MoU) has recently been signed by the government of Kerala to ensure that it will be robots, and not humans, who will now be cleaning sewer holes, bringing the age-old practice of manual scavenging to an end.[15] This MoU is a fitting tribute to Dakshayani's life mission of ridding society of ideas of superiority and negative discrimination.

Notes

1. T. Bhaskaran, *Maharshi Sree Narayana Guru*, Kerala State Bhasha Institute, 2011.

2. Indian Law Commission, *Reports of the Indian Law Commission upon Slavery in India, January 15, 1841; with Appendices*, n.p., 1841, https://catalog.hathitrust.org/Record/008420865 (accessed on 10 July 2018).

3. Charmy Harikrishnan, 'How Dakshayani Velayudhan broke the iron ceiling of caste to become the only Dalit woman in Constituent Assembly', *Economic Times*, 15 August 2017, https://economictimes. indiatimes.com/news/politics-and-nation/how-dakshayani-velayudhan-broke-the-iron-ceiling-of-caste-to-become-the-first-dalit-woman-graduate-of-india/articleshow/60037034. cms?from=mdr (accessed on 10 July 2018).

4. R.K. Kshirsagar, *Dalit Movement in India and Its Leaders, 1857–1956*, M.D. Publications, 1994, p. 362.

5. Swami Vivekananda, *Pearls of Wisdom*, Ramakrishna Mission Institute of Culture, 2010.

6. Ishita Sengupta, 'Dakshayani Velayudhan, the First and the Only Dalit Woman in the Constituent Assembly', *Indian Express*, 19 January 2018, https://indianexpress.com/article/gender/dakshayani-velayudhan-the-first-and-only-dalit-woman-in-the-constituent-assembly-5030932/ (accessed on 14 March 2020).

7. Harikrishnan, 'How Dakshayani Velayudhan Broke the Iron Ceiling of Caste to Become the Only Dalit Woman in Constituent Assembly'.

8. Harihar Swarup, *Power Profiles*, Har-anand Publications Pvt. Ltd, 2010, p. 192.

9. Ruth Manorama, 'Background information on Dalit women in India', Rightlivelihoodaward.org, http://www.rightlivelihoodaward. org/fileadmin/Files/PDF/Literature_Recipients/Manorama/ Background_Manorama.pdf (accessed on 30 January 2020).

10. 'How the only Dalit woman involved in making our Constitution faced sexism during a speech', News Minute, 15 August 2017, https://www.thenewsminute.com/article/how-only-dalit-woman-involved-making-our-constitution-faced-sexism-during-speech-66820 (accessed on 30 January 2020).

11. Dakshayani Velayudhan, speech at the constitutent assembly on 28 August 1947, http://loksabhaph.nic.in/writereaddata/cadebatefiles/ C28081947.html (accessed on 30 January 2020).

12. Harikrishnan, 'How Dakshayani Velayudhan Broke the Iron Ceiling of Caste to Become the Only Dalit Woman in Constituent Assembly'.

13. Dakshayani Velayudhan's speech in the constiutent assembly on 29 November 1948, http://164.100.47.194/loksabha/writereaddata/ cadebatefiles/C29111948.pdf (accessed on 30 January 2020).

14. Manorama, 'Background information on Dalit women in India'.

15. 'Kerala Water Authority to Use Robots for Cleaning Sewer Holes', Kerala Water Authority, https://kwa.kerala.gov.in/kwa/kerala-water-authority-to-use-robots-for-cleaning-sewer-holes/ (accessed on 10 July 2018).

Gurram Jashuva

Poetry is a worthy expression of human emotions and the realities of the world. Poetry reveals more about communities and the experiences of the people, mainstream and marginalized alike, than any official narrative can ever do.

If ever there was a poet and literary icon in India who spoke movingly of the experience of oppression and the horror of untouchability, it was Gurram Jashuva. A revolutionary personality, Jashuva caused a tectonic shift in people's minds and hearts when it came to understanding the vehemence of caste-based discrimination; the experience of poverty and deprivation taught Jashuva humility, and this shone through in his works. He was declared the first modern Telugu Dalit poet,[1] a significant achievement for the Dalit literary movement in Andhra Pradesh and in India as a whole.

Jashuva was born on 28 September 1895 in Vinukonda, a small town in the backward Palnadu region of Guntur in Andhra Pradesh, into a community of leather workers. His father, Veeraiah, was a Golla,[2] a backward but "touchable" caste, and his mother, Lingamamba, was from the untouchable Madiga caste. Both of them were converted Christians, and Veeraiah worked in a church as a pastor. However, he was excommunicated from his caste due to his marriage with an untouchable, and he subsequently spent his life as an untouchable himself. Growing up in poverty and deprivation had a significant impact on Jashuva's life and is palpable in each verse of his poetry.[3]

Jashuva was educated and employed in a Christian missionary school; not many records exist on the grade till which he studied.[4] But after his excommunication from Christianity, because he wrote on themes related to Hindu literature, such as *Dhruva vijayam* (the victory of Dhruva, a great devotee of Lord Vishnu) and *himadhamarka parinayam* (the marriage of Shiva and Parvati), he was thrown out of his job. He not only read Hindu religious scriptures, but also radically questioned certain practices among his fellow Christians, who said that Jashuva's writings contributed to the propagation of Hinduism.

His excommunication from Christianity is recorded by Jashuva in his autobiography, *Naa Katha*, as: 'Those [Christian fathers] who plant the seeds of fear saying that by birth we are all sinners, I lost their confidence, which finally resulted in my excommunication.'[5]

On the other hand, he faced bitter treatment from the Hindu society as well. In one instance, he was humiliated at a gathering of poets in Vinukonda and chased out of the venue. Many upper-caste scholars heckled him as he tried to learn Sanskrit.[6] These simultaneous confrontations with both communities turned him into a rebel, and he devoted his life to challenging the inequalities in society.

Jashuva's childhood was riddled with hardship and hurdles. Hemalatha Lavanam, his daughter, says that he had developed his rebellious attitude towards inequality and the inhuman practice of untouchability from his very childhood. According to her, Jashuva was denied entry into a playground by a Hindu boy. Angered, Jashuva had slapped him and said: 'Brother! This slap is not for you but it is for your caste discrimination.'[7]

This experience of facing vehement caste-based discrimination had a profound effect on Jashuva. In his three-part autobiography *Naa Katha*, he writes how there was discrimination even on the playground—the untouchables were banished from playing alongside upper caste-Hindu children. In Jashuva's words: 'All caste-Hindu boys without any discrimination freely used to play like brothers. By seeing them I used to feel pained.'[8]

But what prompted him to take to poetry? Jashuva's early experiences in his classroom and the extent to which he was inspired by poets such as Thirupathi Venkata Kavulu and Koppurapu Kavulu could have been factors. Jashuva's career as a teacher and his journey as a poet began simultaneously.[9] He wrote in a style that began to be accepted in the mainstream Telugu literary fraternity; the themes he used and the images his words conjured up were sharply critical of the upper castes. Jashuva received public acclaim and literary honours as well. His most famous work is *Gabbilam*, a long poem comprising two parts. Modelled on Kalidasa's famous poem *Meghaduta*, which encapsulates a message sent by an exiled lover to his wife, Jashuva's poem describes a message sent by a poor untouchable man to Lord Shiva in Varanasi. In Kalidasa's poem, the messenger is the cloud, while in *Gabbilam*, the outcaste narrates his plight to a bat and asks the bat to convey his message to Lord Shiva. In the selection of the title, Jashuva draws a similarity between the life of an untouchable and that of a *gabbilam*, or a bat. For Jashuva, a bat, a symbol of a bad omen, was treated as neither a bird nor an animal; similarly, despite being born a human being, an untouchable is not treated as one and is denied even basic human needs and dignity.[10]

Jashuva raised several issues in *Gabbilam*. He was critical of the classical literary tradition and the aberrations in Indian culture that did not accommodate those from the subaltern communities. He portrayed the poor and hungry untouchable as the protagonist in Telugu poetry for the first time. Very significantly, he raised the issue of caste discrimination in the Telugu literary public sphere.

On careful analysis, the essence of *Gabbilam* is the detailing of different aspects of caste-based discrimination and the miserable socio-economic conditions for Dalits then; certain scholars also look at it as a reiteration of the temple-entry movements for Dalits. Jashuva's patriotic strain is also distinctly discernible. In the poem, he describes the untouchable as a son of India:

> In simplicity, content with a penny
> In innocence, forgetful of all troubles,
> In suffering, suppressing hunger,
> Destined to live in penury
> The untouchable,
> This unwanted child,
> Of the great mother,
> Bharat, that is, India.[11]

In 2019 *Gabbilam* was performed as a solo act by Inumula Venkateshwar Rao.[12]

The highlight of Jashuva's struggle and journey as a poet was that he learnt to write in poetic form when it was considered the sole right and monopoly of the upper caste to do so. His creativity lay in conveying everything in poetic form, which he mastered.[13]

Jashuva angered many upper-caste Hindus by venturing into the field of poetry. Some even threatened his life because of this. Many scholars questioned Jashuva's skill as a poet because they could not bring themselves to accept a Dalit learning the art and nuance of poetry, 'By looking at my poetic skills and beauty of its forms he applauded me and enquired about my caste. While knowing my caste, he said Saraswati (goddess of learning or knowledge) got polluted and left the place. I feel pained and humiliated to recount such incidents,' he recounted.[14]

Despite being humiliated by the upper castes, Jashuva persevered and continued to speak through his poetry. Marxist poets such as Sri Sri called him a 'second-rate' poet (*upakavi* in Telugu).[15] However, these hurdles only encouraged him to continue to weave an enduring literary influence on the masses and carve a niche for himself in the Telugu literary world.

Throughout his career, Jashuva donned many hats. He was a poet, a schoolteacher and a playwright in a traditional drama company in Rajahmundry. Later, he also worked as a producer in All India Radio in Madras (now Chennai).[16] As a prolific writer, he has more than thirty-five literary works to his credit.[17] Some of his more famous works are *Gabbilam* (The Bat), *Firadousi* (a story related to a Persian poet who was deceived by a King), *Musafirloo* (A Travelogue), *Mumtaz Mahaloo* (The Love Story of Shah Jahan), *Swapana Katha* (The Story of a Dream).[18] Kashinatha Nageshwara Rao, the founder of *Andhra Patrika* daily newspaper and the *Bharathi* journal and also an active Gandhian, published Jashuva's writings and provided some much-needed financial help in the form of an honorarium for his writings.[19]

Jashuva's life epitomizes knowledge and a clear vision. In his poetry he adopted the *kandakavya style*, which was popular then. His *Aanatha* (*The Orphan*) is one of the best examples of this form when it came to writing about social themes. He also wrote his autobiography *Naa Katha* in the same form. The uniqueness of his poetry, however, was in its original content.

Most of Jashuva's writings were centred on patriotism, revivalism, nature and social reform. He ensured the representation of universal truth, beauty and equality in his *kandakavya*s. In a recent study on Jashuva, R. Chandra Shekar Reddy argued that 'Jashuva's poems are not incomprehensible romantic poems. But, there is death, darkness and tears in Jashuva. When he sees nature, he thinks of the relationship between man and nature. When he sees a woman, he thinks of her hunger, poverty and family.[20]

Firadousi is one of Jashuva's major works. The story is about the Persian poet Firadousi in the court of the sultan Mahmud of Ghazni. According to the story, the king promised the poet a gold coin for every word in a piece of work he commissioned him to write. After the poet spent ten years toiling day and night to create a masterpiece, the king, under the influence of jealous courtiers, reneged on his promise and offered only silver coins. Heartbroken by this breach of trust, the poet committed suicide.[21]

Jashuva's collection, *Baapoojee* (1948), is an expression of his anguish upon hearing of the assassination of Mahatma Gandhi. This collection of fifteen poems that eulogize the life and work of Gandhi show us Jashuva's love and respect for him as he laments Gandhi's death as the country's misfortune.[22] Jashuva was in favour of national liberation from colonial rule and urged his Dalit brethren to take part in the freedom movement. One of his works is also based on the Indian National Army (INA) founder, Netaji Subhas Chandra Bose, titled *Nethaji*.

Jashuva's approach reminds one of Adi Shankaracharya, the exponent of Advaita Vedanta, who worked to ensure that everyone had access to knowledge irrespective of caste, creed and gender. It is said that an incident in Shankaracharya's life tested his own beliefs and led to a rethinking of his own philosophies. After a bath in the Ganga river at Varanasi, as Shankaracharya was proceeding towards the temple of Lord Vishwanath with his disciples, he noticed a person from the Shudra community walking towards him. He immediately asked him to remove himself from his sight and his path. 'But it is you who said that the Absolute is everywhere, and yet you want me to get away from you as if you and I were different,' the person from the Shudra community is said to have retorted. Shankaracharya immediately realized that he had been shown the limits of his own philosophy. The text *Maneesha Panchakam*[23] emerged from this realization, with the strong message that distinctions based on social, moral or ethical divisions did not have place in the teachings of the Upanishads.

Jashuva died on 24 July 1971. He spent his life encouraging in the Dalit community the sensitivity necessary for its empowerment. He tried to ensure that everybody had some access to knowledge and considered education as an important catalyst for empowerment. Following his passion, he challenged social conventions and became a trailblazer in his own right by creating poetry that was widely acclaimed and respected by even his contemporaries.

Even after almost seventy years, the contemporary relevance of Jashuva is discernible in literary circles. *Gabbilam* has been translated into Tamil, which was published by the Hyderabad-based Thiruvalluvar Tamil Sangam.[24] Referred to as Mahakavi, or Navayuga Kavi, Jashuva is a Sahitya Akademi awardee. He also received the Padma Bhushan and was conferred the honorary doctorate of Kala Prapoorna by Andhra University.[25]

Today a memorial exists in his name, and an auditorium is said to be in the pipeline as well. Some other initiatives to remember his legacy by are songs in his name in the digital format,[26] contemporary essay-writing competitions and film festivals by certain organizations.[27] One should also watch out for literary fan clubs that have sprung up to better understand Jashuva's influence on society.[28]

Jashuva's writings emerged from the margins and firmly secured a place in mainstream Telugu literature. He was the only Telugu Dalit poet whose writings were prescribed as textbooks in high schools and universities.[29] Through his writings he not only proved himself a great poet but also overcame the barriers of caste and religion. The following lines capture his personality and achievements eloquently:

> I will not be caged by the web of caste and religious lines
> Whatever the world thinks of me
> It will have no bearing on my existence as a universal human being.[30]

Jashuva fought caste, casteism and untouchability tooth and nail. He considered poverty and caste- and religion-based discrimination as his two teachers. Through his writings, he rebelled for social reformation to be at the heart of universal well-being. He is an example how language can be a great unifier; he understood and learnt languages such as Sanskrit, in addition to being an expert in the Telugu language. Stalwarts such as Gurram Jashuva, among others, have played the role of reformers when discrimination was an everyday reality. He scrubbed away tirelessly at the evils of society so that what shined forth were the brightness, brilliance and richness of a culture that had stood the test of time.

Notes

1. K. Satyanarayana, 'The discovery of Jashuva: the shaping of Dalit literary tradition in Telugu', *Language Forum*, Bahri Publications, Vol. 33, Issue 1, January–June 2007.

2. Golla is a backward caste in Andhra Pradesh. In caste hierarchy, it is placed under the Shudras and is considered a touchable caste. For more details, see E. Thurston's and K. Rangachari's *Castes and Tribes of Southern India* (Madras: Government Press, 1909), pp. 284–96. According to them, the social status of a Golla was fairly high—they were allowed to mix freely with the Kapu, Kamma, Balija and other Shudra castes. Brahmins would take buttermilk from their hands. The hereditary occupation of a Golla was tending sheep, cattle and selling milk (pp. 184–5).

3. G.A. Oddie, 'Christian Conversion in the Telugu Country, 1860-1900: A Case Study of One Protestant Movement in the Godavery-Krishna Delta', *Sage Journals*, 1 January 1975.

4. Chinnaiah Jangam, 'Desecrating the sacred taste: The making of Gurram Jashua—the father of Dalit literature in Telugu', *Indian Economic and Social History Review*, vol. 51, no. 2, 2014, pp. 177–98.

5. Ibid.

6. Id.

7. Id.

8. Id.

9. Id.

10. Id.

11. Id.

12. 'Telugu poet Gurram Jashuva remembered by literary fans on his 124th birth anniversary', *News Minute*, 28 September 2019, https://www.thenewsminute.com/article/telugu-poet-gurram-jashuva-remembered-literary-fans-his-124th-birth-anniversary-109660 (accessed on 11 March 2020).

13. Jangam, 'Desecrating the sacred taste: The making of Gurram Jashua—the father of Dalit literature in Telugu'.

14. Ibid.

15. Id.

16. Id.

17. Id.

18. Id.

19. Id.

20. K. Satyanarayana, 'The Discovery of Jashuva: The Shaping of Dalit Literary Tradition in Telugu', *Language Forum*, Bahri Publications, vol. 33, no. 1, January–June 2007.

21. Jangam, 'Desecrating the sacred taste: The making of Gurram Jashua—the father of Dalit literature in Telugu'.

22. Ibid.

23. Swami Chinmayananda, *Maneesha Panchakam*, Chinmaya Prakashan, 1993.

24. M.T. Saju, 'Red poem Gabbilam takes Tamil avatar after 70 years', *Times of India*, 2 October 2012, https://timesofindia.indiatimes.com/city/chennai/Red-poem-Gabbilam-takes-Tamil-avatar-after-70-years/articleshow/16634293.cms (accessed on 11 March 2020).

25. 'Telugu poet Gurram Jashuva remembered by literary fans on his 124th birth anniversary', The News Minute, 28 September 2019, https://www.thenewsminute.com/article/telugu-poet-gurram-jashuva-remembered-literary-fans-his-124th-birth-anniversary-109660 (accessed on 11 March 2020).

26. Ibid.

27. 'Essay contest to mark Telugu poet Gurram Jashuva's 125th birth anniversary', *New Indian Express*, 11 September 2019, https://www.newindianexpress.com/cities/vijayawada/2019/sep/11/essay-contest-to-mark-telugu-poet-gurram-jashuvas-125th-birth-anniversary-2031947.html (accessed on 11 March 2020); 'Short film festival In memory of Gurram Jashuva at Chukkapalli Pitchiah

auditorium in Vijayawada', Hans India, 27 September 2018, https://www.thehansindia.com/posts/index/Andhra-Pradesh/2018-09-27/Short-film-festival-In-memory-of-Gurram-Jashuva-at-Chukkapalli-Pitchiah-auditorium-in-Vijayawada/414393 (accessed on 11 March 2020).

28. 'Telugu poet Gurram Jashuva remembered by literary fans on his 124th birth anniversary', News Minute, 28 September 2019, https://www.thenewsminute.com/article/telugu-poet-gurram-jashuva-remembered-literary-fans-his-124th-birth-anniversary-109660 (accessed on 11 March 2020).

29. Jangam, 'Desecrating the sacred taste: The making of Gurram Jashua—the father of Dalit literature in Telugu'.

30. Ibid.

Guru Ravidas

The experience of oppression, especially when linked to one's background or identity, can lead to deep bitterness, even apathy. But when the focus is shifted to devotion and dedication, that pain transforms into gain. This is where Guru Ravidas deserves mention. A Dalit hero, social reformer and a philosopher, he rewrote the script of oppression by responding to social injustice with devotion and dignity,[1] but without dismissing the struggle of the people and without massaging the ego of the elite. In fact, he countered the latter's weakness of character by values and virtues, shining a spotlight on their hypocrisy, an effective remedy for their stubborn discrimination.

Ravidas (sometimes referred to as Ravidass and Raidas) was born in Seer Govardhanpur, near the sacred town of Varanasi. A popular belief is that he lived in the fifteenth and the sixteenth centuries,[2] and died at the age of 121; he is said to have married Mata Lona at a young age and had a son named Vijaydas. His parents' names were Santokh Das and Kalsi Devi.[3] One account also states that he lived for 151 years.[4] Ravidas's birth anniversary is celebrated on Magh Purnima (full-moon day in the Hindu month of Magh, in the month of January–February as per the

Gregorian calendar) every year at Shri Guru Ravidass Janam Sthan Mandir in Seer Govardhanpur with great pomp. Lakhs of devotees visit this sacred temple to pay their obeisance.[5] Today the temple is a symbol of Dalit identity and Dalit awakening.[6] It is also referred to as 'Begumpura', which Ravidas had said would be a city with no discrimination, which everyone would be allowed to frequent freely.[7]

Ravidas belonged to the Chamar community, who are traditionally cobblers, and his family's profession was leather tanning, shoemaking and shoe repair.[8] Employing the use of dead animal skin was seen as untouchable work. As his work needed him to supply footwear to renunciates and ascetics, he was exposed to their transformational teachings and spent a lot of time in spiritual pursuit. He would go on to call himself 'a tanner set free'.[9]

One of the remarkable achievements of Ravidas was that he started dressing like the upper caste Brahmins and adopting some of their rituals. He would blow the conch, ring temple bells and apply a tilak on his forehead. The opposition he faced was enormous but it did not prevent him from continuing to do what he was doing.[10]

Once, when upper-caste priests tried to stop Ravidas from even worshipping in the temple, he responded with words centred on devotion and love, 'Listen, friends, it is not important what I am or what you are. High or low is just your invention, only love and devotion please the lord.'[11]

People of the subaltern communities faced grim oppression and brutal treatment by those who believed that religious practice was the birthright of only the upper castes. What set Ravidas apart from his contemporaries who stood up for the downtrodden was his wisdom, his compassion for all mankind and his unruffled focus. He made efforts to educate the common man on spiritual and social messages that found expression in his beautiful words. He uplifted society by uplifting the state of mind of people, the oppressors and the oppressed alike.[12]

Ravidas studied under Pandit Sharda Nand. Despite hailing from an upper caste, the latter taught Ravidas, for whom he had great regard. If Sharda Nand taught him only a few letters, Ravidas transformed them into poetic lines.[13]

One of the most captivating aspects of Ravidas's life was that many kings and queens yearned to learn from him, among them Queen Jhali, also known as Jhalan Bai of Chittorgarh. It is said that she first went to Kabir but then sought initiation from Ravidas. She was ridiculed for seeking initiation from a Chamar but that did not stop her from learning from Ravidas.[14] Apart from her, another prominent individual who sought initiation from Ravidas included Raja Pipa (Malwa, Rajasthan). Some historical accounts state that some kings and queens even built temples in his name, which were later demolished and converted into other places of worship.[15]

Kabir Das was Ravidas's contemporary, considered an elder brother and guru by him. A story that can only be called bizarre goes that to voice their protest against Ravidas as he worshipped the saligram in temples and taught kings and queens, the upper castes started killing themselves in front of Ravidas. Deeply shaken, he sought advice from Kabir on how to handle them. But Kabir was only too sure that no matter what they did, they would not listen, as they all considered themselves upper castes. However, a saligram is said to have spoken, 'Raidās is my genuine devotee, and false are those Brahmins who pester him.'[16]

Ravidas was so close to Kabir that when he received an invitation from Queen Jhalan Bai to visit Chittorgarh, he is said to have consulted him for advice on whether to go or to just send a letter instead—to which, Kabir vehemently insisted that he go in person.[17] Another significant event was a meeting in Varanasi between Ravidas, Kabir and Guru Nanak, in which they discussed ways to attain social equality and means to raise opposition to any atrocity committed against the lower castes.[18]

Ravidas was a towering figure of his times, who not only sought truth but revelled in its bliss. He was the perfect embodiment of mission and vision—his mission was the upliftment of the masses, and his vision was purity of the idea of oneness. This translated into harmony and equality. He took tragedies in his stride and used peace as a social weapon to fight false norms. Our society is richer today thanks to his contributions to the Bhakti movement and his poetry, devotional songs and scriptures. Many of these have become dicta for Dalits of Punjab and other places. So much so that Prime Minister Narendra Modi, in a Twitter post in 2017, acknowledged his massive contribution to society. He tweeted: 'Guru Ravidas' pure thoughts and ideals have had a profound impact on society. He emphasised on values of harmony, equality & compassion, which are central to India's culture & ethos.'[19]

Ravidas initiated a new alphabet, Gurmukhi, consisting of thirty-four letters, to convey his thoughts in a simple and conversational way, since the Devanagari script was inaccessible to the lower castes due to social prejudices.[20] Before the partition of India and Pakistan, a Lahore court had adjudicated that the Gurmukhi alphabet was coined by Guru Ravidas.[21] The Sikh Bani, or Sikh teachings, are also in Gurmukhi. After forty-one poems by Ravidas were compiled by Guru Arjan Dev in the Guru Granth Sahib, he earned the title 'Guru', whereas earlier he was just known as Bhagat Ravidas.

He is also considered to be the spiritual guru of Meerabai, daughter of a king and queen of Rajasthan and a saint in her own right. While she is popularly known to be devoted to Lord Krishna, Guru Ravidas also had a tremendous influence on her.

In her own words:

I kept searching for the secret
Of that Realm but none could reveal it.
When Sant Ravidas, my Master, I met,
He gave my soul the clue
To that Eternal Abode.

Then I ascended and met my Beloved;
And my anguish was finally allayed.

When Ravidas, the perfect Master, I met
The severed twig joined again the tree.
My Master revealed the secret of the Name,
The flame of Meera merged into the Flame.[22]

Just as in Meerabai's songs, the goal in Ravidas's poems is to lose oneself in the ocean of one's devotion.

The saints of Ravidas's time would travel extensively. It is said that Mardana, who used to live with Guru Nanak, would sing the songs of Ravidas on his master's request, such was his regard for the great poet. Like Guru Nanak, Ravidas is known to have shared mystical and miraculous occurrences with his disciples.

Ravidas's following grew without his trying to force his beliefs on anybody. He was kind and non-violent, and made gentle but bold social statements to those in power. His poetic words exhorted the dignity of labour, be it any kind.

Ravidas was undeterred by the hostility he received and continued with the same sincerity and reverence. Fame was quick to follow, but even as the number of his followers grew, Ravidas never quit his profession, that of a cobbler. He cared little for the fact that it was scorned and, instead, reiterated his belief that selfless work would take him closer to his spiritual goals.

Five centuries before the famous 'I have a dream' speech by Martin Luther King Jr, Ravidas envisioned a social utopia through his composition *Begumpura* (literally the 'city without sorrow').[23] He spoke of a peaceful place of equality and humanity, free from the barriers of caste, class and poverty. Some of the same ideas were later echoed in the Constitution of India, drafted by another champion of the downtrodden Dalits, B.R. Ambedkar. However, despite *Begumpura* being a far cry from reality even today, Ravidas's spiritual vision has permeated society deeper, wider and vaster than what most can fathom.

Ravidas was a passionate and extensive traveller, visiting places including Hyderabad, Bhopal, Jodhpur, Ajmer and Bombay (now Mumbai). It is also believed that he also travelled to several countries, such as Saudi Arabia, Iran and Kuwait.[24]

Ravidasia Dera is a religious group of followers in Punjab that is similar in nature and structure to Sikhism.[25] In 2010, Ravidasias (followers of Ravidas) launched their own religion, the Ravidassia Dharam. They set up their own scripture, the Amritbani Satguru Ravidas Maharaj, and also decided on the holiest place of pilgrimage for the community, the Varanasi-based Ravidas Janamsthan Mandir. This place, as mentioned earlier, is also referred to as Begumpura. Various processions and marches from Jalandhar in Punjab to Varanasi in Uttar Pradesh have become central to the Ravidasia identity.[26]

It is said that beyond the forty compositions by Ravidas that are included in the Guru Granth Sahib, there are 200 other works that have been included in Amritbani Satguru Ravidas Maharaj.[27]

One of the biggest tributes to Ravidas is the temple that Babu Jagjivan Ram built for him in Varanasi. It is designed so that four of its spires, one at each corner, represent major religious traditions, while the central fifth tower represents a universal religion, the faith Ravidas believed in and preached.[28]

Ravidas's profound teachings and his immense contribution to Indian society, which shaped an entire era, can only be celebrated by dedicating ourselves to his vision of unity and integration. The values of love, respect and forgiveness that won the hearts of his contemporaries hold true even today, if given a chance to work.

Notes

1. Winand M. Callewaert, *The Hagiographies of Anantadas: The Bhakti Poets of North India*, Routledge, 2000, p. 383.
2. Kuldeep Kumar, 'Seeking a city without sorrow', *Hindu*, 12 September 2019, https://www.thehindu.com/books/books-authors/seeking-a-city-without-sorrow/article29398696.ece (accessed on 12 March 2020).
3. Chain Ram Suman, *Miracles of Satguru Ravidass Ji*, Shri Guru Ravidass Janam Sthan Mandir.
4. Ibid., p. 50.
5. Id., p. 53.
6. Id., p. 55.
7. Id., p. 70.
8. Id., p. 94.
9. John Stratton Hawley and Vasudha Narayanan, eds, *The Life of Hinduism*, University of California Press, 2006, p. 214.
10. Ram Suman, *Miracles of Satguru Ravidass Ji*, p. 95.
11. Callewaert, *The Hagiographies of Anantadas: The Bhakti Poets of North India*, p. 379.
12. Ibid.
13. Ram Suman, *Miracles of Satguru Ravidass Ji*, pp. 108–09.
14. Ibid., pp. 387–9.
15. Id., p. 97.
16. Callewaert, *The Hagiographies of Anantadas: The Bhakti Poets of North India*, p. 393.
17. Ibid., p. 398.
18. Ram Suman, *Miracles of Satguru Ravidass Ji*, pp. 159–160.
19. Twitter, 10 February 2017, https://twitter.com/narendramodi/status/829872090706747392?ref_src=twsrcper%20cent5Etfwper%20cent7Ctwcampper%20cent5Etweetembedper%20cent7Ctwtermper%20cent5E829872090706747392&ref_url=httpsper%20cent3Aper%20cent2Fper%20cent2Fwww.inuth.comper%20cent2Findiaper%20cent2Fhis-ideals-have-a-profound-impact-on-society-prime-minister-narendra-modi-on-guru-ravidas-birth-anniversaryper%20-cent2F (accessed on 12 March 2020).

20. Ram Suman, *Miracles of Satguru Ravidass Ji*, p. 107.
21. Ibid.
22. V.K. Sethi, *Mira: The Divine Lover*, Radha Soami Satsang Beas, 1979.
23. Hawley and Narayanan, eds, *The Life of Hinduism*, University of California Press, 2006, p. 214.
24. Ram Suman, *Miracles of Satguru Ravidass Ji*, p. 154.
25. Guru Prakash and Sudarshan Ramabadran, 'A journey of hope amidst despair', Millennium Post, 11 February 2017, http://www.millenniumpost.in/opinion/news-183662 (accessed on 31 March 2020).
26. Anna Bochkovskaya, 'Begumpura Yatras: Constructing the Ravidassia pilgrimage tradition', *International Journal of Religious Tourism and Pilgrimage*, vol. 4, no. 6, 2016, https://arrow.tudublin.ie/cgi/viewcontent.cgi?article=1163&context=ijrtp (accessed on 12 March 2020).
27. I.P. Singh, 'Punjab sect declares new religion', *Times of India*, 1 February 2010, https://timesofindia.indiatimes.com/india/Punjab-sect-declares-new-religion/articleshow/5521656.cms (accessed on 12 March 2020).
28. John Stratton Hawley, *Three Bhakti Voices: Mirabai, Surdas and Kabir in Their Times and Ours*, Oxford University Press India, 2012, p. 334.

Kabir Das

Mark Twain beautifully said of Varanasi that it is '. . . older than history, older than tradition, older even than legend, and looks twice as old as all of them put together'.[1]

Indian civilization has always found rejuvenation in Varanasi, which has produced some incredible social and spiritual reformers whose works have stood the test of time. These reformers played an important role in readapting Hinduism for people while rejecting the ritualized classical approach to it. In this context, one needs to remember one of India's biggest spiritual leader and mystic poet–singers, Kabir Das, a cotton weaver from Varanasi.

Kabir, which means 'great',[2] had an enormous impact on his times. His words were unforgettable. Within a century of his death, people were writing his words down hundreds of miles away, in Rajasthan and Punjab.[3] Bharat Ratna Ambedkar has also mentioned Kabir as one of his most significant forebearers.[4]

At the outset, we must state that the birth and death of Kabir has been shrouded in mystery. Scholars on Kabir have many times had to rely on autobiographical lines to understand his relevance, impact and message. Historian Hazari Prasad Dwivedi has placed Kabir's birth in 1399 and death in 1515, at the age of 119. Another strand of biographical thought is propagated by the Kabir Panthis (a mixed community of ascetics and householders),[5] who claim that Kabir lived for 300 years, between 1205 and 1505.[6]

One of Kabir's disciples, Sri Ananta Das, wrote the 'Kabir Parichai' sometime in the second half of the fifteenth century, documenting important events in Kabir's life. This is perhaps the nearest authentic evidence to the life of Kabir. Surprisingly, in this, the date or year of his birth is not mentioned. However, what is established is that he was a weaver, lived in Kashi, was a contemporary of King Veer Singh Dev, that Sikandar Lodi tortured him, forcing him to shift to Magahar out of fear, that he died in Magahar at the age of 120, and that he was a disciple of the poet Ramananda.[7]

Apart from this, there are two other important pieces of work that throw light on Kabir—saint Nabhadas's *Bhaktamal*, composed after 1600, and the Sikh Kirtarpur Bir, written in 1604.[8]

One story about his birth is that the newborn Kabir was found on the side of a large pond at Lahartara near Kashi by a childless weaver couple, Neeru and Neema. This place where he was found was subsequently called 'Kabir Chaura',[9] which played a pivotal role in his life, as this is where he played, sang and, later, even delivered his discourses. Kabir was deeply inclined towards spirituality and found answers in balanced living.

Kabir is famously known to have helped the common man understand the philosophical core of spirituality and been critical of the all-consuming need in religion for rituals. Credit is truly due to such a reformer who repivoted the spiritual compass of civilization by reiterating the need for a balanced and harmonious mind and underlining how God was within humans themselves.

Kabir's contribution to the Indian spiritual movement lay in how he dealt directly with the common man—his words were directed at the seeker. Kabir himself did not write or compile any book—what he sang and taught through verses and couplets stayed with his listeners and disciples, and was subsequently compiled by them into *Beejak*. This had three distinct parts *ramaini*, *shabad* and *sakhi*.[10]

Kabir's words were primarily in two literary formats—the rhymed couplet (known as *doha*, *sakhi* or *shalok*) and lyric poems (*shabda*, *shabad*, *pad* or *bhajan*), in addition to the ramaini and folk-song forms[11]. The lyric poems, commonly known as bhajans, vary in meter and are usually six to eighteen lines in length, while the couplets comprise four half-lines.[12]

Research scholars have also claimed that there are twenty-one poetic works of Kabir that his disciples compiled—*Sukh Nidhan, Gorakh Goshit, Kabir Panji, Balakh ki Ramaini, Anand Ram Sagar, Ramanand ki Goshti, Shabdawali, Mangal, Basant, Holi, Rekhati, Jhoolan, Kakahara, Hindol, Barahamasa, Chanchar, Chautisi, Alifnama, Ramaini, Sakhi* and *Beejak*. However, some scholars believe that Kabir's disciples have included some of their own works in this list.[13]

Two questions that come to mind when we think of Kabir are: Whom did Kabir learn from; and despite hailing from a lower caste of weavers, did the saints of his time accept him as one of them?

Going with the records available, it is safe to say that Kabir, with his single-minded devotion to Rama, was accepted by all sections of society as a saint. However, he constantly challenged preconceived notions and rituals around religion and was forthright in his criticism of both Hindus and Muslims for their adherence to these. In one instance, he asks a Muslim man—'*Din bhar roja rahat hain, rati hanat hain gaya, yeh to koon, woh vandagi, kaise khoosi khudaya?*', meaning 'You observe a fast during the day and butcher cows at night; this is worship and that is murder. How can one be happy?'[14] In the same vein he criticized Hindus for their meaningless rituals too—'*Moond muraya hari milen, sab koi leyee maraya, bar-bar ke murate, bhera na baikuntha jaya*', meaning 'If one can enter heaven only by getting one's head shaved, then all should get their heads shaved. By getting shaved many times, the sheep do not go to heaven.'[15]

Kabir always stressed the oneness of the gods, be it Rama or Rehman. He said that every individual had their own relationship with God and that they were God's living forms; in essence, he said, God was within the physical self. To this effect, Kabir said, 'Moko kahān dhundho bande, main to tere pās mein' (where are you searching for me, I'm within you).[16]

Kabir fought casteism in unique ways. Legend has it that once, when he was dining with upper-caste saints in south India, the latter demanded that Kabir sit in a separate line because of his caste—and if he did want to sit with them, he would have to recite lines from the Vedas. In response, Kabir asked the buffalo he had brought with him to recite the lines on his behalf, and the animal immediately did so. At this, the upper-caste saints sought Kabir's forgiveness and let him sit with them.[17]

Another story relates how Kabir met and brought about the spiritual transformation of Shah Ibrahim Adham of Balk (now in Afghanistan). Legend has it that Shah Ibrahim wanted to have a vision of God, and so he called all the sadhus and fakirs of his kingdom to his court. But when none of them could do his bidding, he had them jailed. Soon after, Kabir appeared in court and sought the release of the jailed sadhus and fakirs. However, Shah Ibrahim flatly refused and insisted that Kabir show him a vision of God. Kabir agreed but demanded the release first. When Shah Ibrahim asked Kabir how he could be trusted, the latter just placed his hand on his buffalo, and the animal spoke that Kabir was telling the truth. Similar other incidents that transpired between Shah Ibrahim and Kabir led Ibrahim to become Kabir's disciple.[18]

There is another story that relates how Kabir taught Ibrahim humility. Legend has it that when Ibrahim sought initation from Kabir, the latter refused. But Ibrahim persisted, listening to Kabir's discourses whenever he got the chance. The more he did so, the more he sought initiation. Kabir then acceded to the request, but on condition that Ibrahim work as his servant. So for almost twelve years, Ibrahim served Kabir and was then initiated as his disciple. This is how Kabir taught him to be humble, to serve others and to be one with all.[19]

However, what remains inconclusive about Kabir is whether he was married and had children. Two accounts that we came across alluded to him being married. While one named Kabir's wife as Loi, the other source did not mention her by any name.[20] Kabir's children were named Kamal and Kamali. Some scholars have also pointed out that Kabir in his poetic works alludes to the essence of marital life. However, there are other versions that state Kabir continued to lead the life of an ascetic; no authentic evidence exists to confirm whether Kabir was married or not.

Another defining feature of Kabir's contribution to society was his association with the Guru Granth Sahib. But did he ever meet Guru Nanak?

Guru Nanak and Kabir, according to prevailing oral accounts, had met each other during their lifetimes. A *Janam Sakhi*, written in the Gurmukhi script, depicts Kabir as Nanak's main source of inspiration. The Guru Granth Sahib consists of hymns by Sikh gurus, along with works by Hindu and Muslim saints, including Kabir. Of all the *bhagat*s, or holy Sikh men, and Sufis whose works are included, Kabir's contribution—of 541 poems—is the largest.[21]

A lot has been written about Kabir's shifting to Magahar from Kashi. There are multiple versions of the circumstances under which this happened. One says Kabir wished to challenge the then popular idea that death at Kashi ensured redemption whereas death at Magahar ensured rebirth as a donkey. Another states Kabir moved to Magahar because he wanted to escape torture by Sikander Lodi. Every time Lodi visited Kashi he showed extreme cruelty towards Kabir because he attracted a faithful following of both Hindus and Muslims.

The disciples and devotees of Kabir were from many regions. Reconstruction of the history of Kabirpanth, a philosophy based on the teachings of Kabir, has proven difficult because studies have reiterated that the panth is comprised of only oral traditions. The evolution of Kabirpanthis has been observed roughly since the seventeenth century, at least in some parts of central and northern India. As per a conservative estimate by scholars and sect followers, it currently has about three million followers in India alone, spread across the states of Bihar, Chhattisgarh, Jharkhand, Odisha, Rajasthan, Himachal Pradesh, Uttarakhand, Punjab, Jammu, Uttar Pradesh, Madhya Pradesh, Gujarat, Maharashtra and Nagaland.[22]

Kabir also has followers outside India, in neighbouring and Caribbean countries.[23] As a case in point, in the early twentieth century, the *samadhi mandir* (where Kabir left his mortal remains) at the Kabir Chaura in Varanasi is also believed to have received funds from his followers and devotees in Fiji and Mauritius, with which it initially got constructed.[24]

When Acharya Kshitimohan Sen of Vishva-Bharati, Santiniketan, published his collection of Kabir's verses in Bengali, he drew upon the poet's verses passed down as oral tradition and not in any manuscript. This left an impact on one of the greatest literary minds of the time, Rabindranath Tagore—so much so that he translated a hundred verses from it. These were published in 1914 in London as *One Hundred Poems of Kabir*. Kabir was the only poet, apart from himself, Tagore ever translated,[25] and the latter maintained throughout that Kabir was a modern and not a medieval poet.

Popular media has also played a role in contemporizing Kabir and helping spread his messages to the masses. Numerous films and documentaries have been made in the past decade; four films by Shabnam Virmani as part of the Kabir Project are especially noteworthy. There are also annual Kabir festivals held in India and abroad. The Kabir Festival Mumbai brings together singers, dancers, storytellers and filmmakers to share Kabir's works through the arts. The poet-saint even has a strong presence in Bollywood, especially through its music.[26]

Casteism is an evil that needs holistic intervention to be rooted out from the society. Kabir was one of the few figures in history to have participated in such intervention. While he was unable to break down the caste structure in India, Kabir did inspire numerous people to reorganize themselves outside of it and realize the presence of God within.[27] And he did so by retaining the principles of tolerance, equality and plurality.[28]

In a society that is now characterized by scientific and technological advancement more than ever before, there is undoubtedly the need for a more equitable social order. This reorganization will require the efforts of numerous stakeholders—the media, civil society, the judiciary, spiritual organizations and the younger generation. It is imperative that these efforts not only be unified, but also follow the basic tenets of Kabir's teaching of tolerance—encapsulated perfectly in his following iconic doha:

> Stood in a marketplace,
> Kabir wishes all well.
> Looking neither for a friend,
> nor an enemy.[29]

Kabir was a critical insider within the Indian intellectual tradition. Yes, the Dalit narrative today is replete with agony, victimhood and protest, but on the other hand, there are icons such as Kabir, who tried to alleviate the woes of the common man throughout his life. It is testimony to his greatness and reach that some today remember him as God, some as an incarnation of God, some as a devotee of Prince Rama, some as a spiritual guide, yet others as a Bhakti poet and a great social reformer.

Notes

1. Diana. L. Eck, *Banaras: City of Light*, Columbia University Press, 1999.
2. John Stratton Hawley, *Three Bhakti Voices: Mirabai, Surdas and Kabir in Their Times and Ours*, Oxford University Press India, 2012, p. 279.
3. Ibid., p. 268.
4. Id., p. 276.
5. Id., p. 269.
6. Shrikant Prasoon, *Knowing Sant Kabir: Life and Teachings*, Hindoology Books, 2012, p. 29.
7. Ibid., p. 27.
8. Hawley, *Three Bhakti Voices*, p. 280.
9. Prasoon, *Knowing Sant Kabir*, p. 45.
10. Ibid.
11. 'Educational Insight: The Mystic Mind and Music of Kabir', Hinduism Today, July-August-September 2016, https://www.hinduismtoday.com/modules/smartsection/item.php?itemid=5705 (accessed on 31 March 2020).
12. Linda Hess, 'Three Kabir Collections: A Comparative Study', *The Sants: Studies in a Devotional Tradition of India*, eds Karine Schomer and W.H. McLeod, Berkeley Religious Studies Series, 1987, p. 113.
13. Prasoon, *Knowing Sant Kabir*, p. 33.
14. Ibid., p. 40.
15. Ibid., p. 41.
16. Id., p. 64.
17. David N. Lorenzen, *Kabir Legends and Ananta-Das's Kabir Parachai*, State University of New York Press, 1991, p. 66.
18. Ibid., p. 67.
19. Prasoon, *Knowing Sant Kabir*, p. 50.
20. Lorenzen, *Kabir Legends and Ananta-Das's* Kabir Parachai, p. 50.
21. Purnendu Ranjan, 'Reconsturction of the History of Kabirpanth, a Devotional Sect Active in North and Central India', *Proceedings of the Indian History Congress*, vol. 72, part I, 2011, pp. 491–500.
22. Ibid.
23. Id.

24. Prasoon, *Knowing Sant Kabir*, p. 47.
25. Anshu Tandon, 'Reading Kabir: A Short History', Swarajya, 20 June 2016, https://swarajyamag.com/culture/reading-kabir-a-short-history (accessed on 31 March 2020).
26. S. Rajam, 'Educational Insight: The Mystic Mind and Music of Kabir', Hinduism Today, July–September 2016, https://www.hinduismtoday.com/modules/smartsection/item.php?itemid=5705 (accessed on 31 March 2020).
27. Rekha Pande, 'The Social Context of the Bhakti Movement: A Study in Kabir', *Proceedings of Indian History Congress*, January 1985, vol. 46, pp. 230–35.
28. Ibid.
29. Ahmad Shah, *The Bijak (Or the Complete Works) of Kabir*, Low Price Publications, reprint edition, 2011.

Kanshiram

It is rare to see Dalit leaders given honorifics such as Manyavar, Saheb and Bahujan Nayak,[1] but Kanshiram was a unique leader of his times, under whose vision the Dalit community could carve out a niche for itself in the national political arena.

In the contemporary political stage in India today, many tend to miss the nuances that Kanshiram brought to the fore, specifically in bringing together the subaltern communities as a strong political force in his time. He was a rare political entrepreneur, who was much ahead of his times. He founded the Bahujan Samaj Party (BSP) by imagining a vote bank comprising all the backward communities, including the other backward classes (OBC), the scheduled castes (SCs), the scheduled tribes (STs) and other minorities, collectively referred to as the 'bahujan samaj'. He was also responsible for coming up with the idea of 'Manuvadi', or the follower of Manu Samhita, as the 'other' or the opponent against whom he would battle.[2] Kanshiram's main aim through the BSP was to bring about social transformation through Dalit empowerment. However, despite contesting against V.P. Singh in Allahabad in 1987 for the first time, it was only in 1991 that he managed to enter the Lok Sabha, when he contested from Ettawah in Uttar Pradesh.[3]

Kanshiram, considered the messaiah of Dalits after Ambedkar, was born on 15 March 1934 in a Dalit Chamar family in the Pirthipur Bunga village, Khawaspur, in the Ropar district of Punjab.[4] He grew up with a love for sports, especially kabaddi and wrestling. Kanshiram studied at the government primary school in Malkapur, which was 2 kilometres from his village. Here he experienced the discrimination that Dalit children faced, such as having different pots for drinking water. Kanshiram was then moved to Islamiya School and the DAV Public School, where he completed his education. He graduated in 1956 with a BSc degree from the government college in Ropar. Kanshiram then went to the staff college in Dehradun for higher studies, where he also prepared for the Public Service Commission exams and worked with the Geological Survey of India. In 1957, Kanshiram joined the High Energy Materials Research Laboratory (renamed the Explosives Research and Development Laboratory in 1960) in Poona (now Pune) as a research assistant.[5]

After working there for five years, his life changed course due to one incident. The laboratory used to be closed on Buddha and Ambedkar jayantis. However, his upper-caste colleagues replaced these two days with jayantis for Bal Gangadhar Tilak and Gopal Krishna Gokhale. The lower-caste staff members were against this move but did not have courage to protest. But with the help of a Class IV employee, Kanshiram took the matter to the then defence minister, Yashwantrao Chavan, who ordered an inquiry into the matter and the two days were reinstated.[6]

It is at this point in his life that Kanshiram started reading the works of social reformers like Mahatma Jyotiba Phule and Ambedkar, which made him understand upper-caste hegemony more clearly and realize that the country's administration comprised only 15 per cent of its entire population. He later understood that unless Dalits consolidated themselves into a single community, they would fail at staking a claim to India's governance and administration.[7]

He resigned from his job and joined the Republican Party of India and also formed the Minority Communities Employees Association.[8] Soon after, his political career began, with the Dalit Shoshit Samaj Sangharsh Samiti (also known as DS-4) and the All-India Backward and Minority Communities Employees Federation (BAMCEF), which had the slogan: 'Become educated, become consolidated and struggle.'[9] He later went on to form the BSP on 14 April 1984. Kanshiram looked at the BAMCEF and the DS-4 as think tanks for the formation of the BSP.

Kanshiram travelled extensively within the country to talk about the cause he stood for and the sociopolitical mission that he had armed himself with. In one of his interviews, he says he has criss-crossed the country at least twice.[10] He also travelled to Japan, Malaysia and the United Kingdom to espouse social equity and the emancipation of Dalits.

With the passage of time and with the growing popularity of DS-4 and the BAMCEF, Kanshiram realized that the creation of a political platform was the next step to ensuring political representation of the Dalits and the backward communities. The BSP was launched in 1984, on the birth anniversary of Ambedkar, 14 April.[11] This is when, for the first time since Independence, reservation for the OBCs was being discussed by the Mandal Commission. In 1979, the Morarji Desai–government set up the Mandal Commission to identify backward classes and address caste-based discrimination. The Commission recommended 27 per cent reservation for OBCs for jobs under the central government and public-sector undertakings. Kanshiram seized the opportunity and galvanized the Dalits and the OBCs as a consolidated political force. The BSP led the pro-Mandal movement. Thousands of party workers, including young men, women and senior citizens, courted arrest in these demonstrations. The All India Revolt against Political Slavery[12] was a movement that was launched in the same year as a platform to unify the OBCs and Dalits to help them realize their political worth as a formidable voting bloc. Needless to say, the BSP had the required momentum and, fortunately for the party, the general elections were announced in 1984. Kanshiram's efforts bore fruit in the electoral performance of a nascent BSP in Uttar Pradesh. The BSP, then barely a year old, contested from nine states and three union territories, and got a formidable 10 lakh votes in the general elections that year, of which more than 6 lakh votes were polled by the party in Uttar Pradesh alone. Kanshiram realized that Uttar Pradesh, when it was undivided, used to send the highest number of MPs to the Lower House and performing well in the state was going to be the perfect example of capturing political power through social engineering.

There are also several reasons behind Kanshiram's selection of Uttar Pradesh, and not Punjab, as his *karmabhoomi* (chosen place of work). First, caste-based discrimination was not as pronounced in Punjab as it was in Uttar Pradesh then. On the other hand, Punjab has also had a number of social-reform movements, given the prevalence of Sikhism in the state. As of 2011, Punjab had the highest population of SCs, constituting 29 per cent in the country. There are thirty-seven loosely organized caste groups within the Dalit community in the state, many of which refuse to be clubbed together.[13] Although Kanshiram did try to galvanize a movement in Punjab through the BSP, unfortunately he could not achieve what he had set out to do—galvanize the bahujan samaj as a strong political force.[14] On the other hand, the Dalits in Punjab had improved their economic situation through jobs. It was Uttar Pradesh where identity was strongly based on social origin. The Jatavs were dominant among the SCs, constituting 54.23 per cent of the total SC population.[15]

Kanshiram wrote a book in 1982 called *The Chamcha Age: An Era of the Stooges*,[16] in which he laid out the philosophical foundation

of the BSP. By *chamcha* he meant the Dalit leaders in mainstream
political parties who, in his opinion, were compromising the
interests of the community to forward their personal political
careers. In a no-holds-barred attack, Kanshiram says:

> After the sad demise of Babasaheb Dr. B.R. Ambedkar in
> 1956, tools, agents and stooges of the high caste Hindus are
> found in abundance, not only in the political field but also in
> every field of human activity and relationship. Initially these
> tools, agents, and stooges were visible only to Dr. Ambedkar
> and the discerning eyes. Later, they were to be detected by the
> intelligentsia. But today, these tools, agents, and stooges are
> so much a common factor of daily life, that they can be easily
> detected by the common man in public. The common man has
> his own terminology. In his terminology, a tool, an agent, or a
> stooge is termed as Chamcha. And in this book, I have decided
> to use the common man's terminology. To my mind, it will be
> fruitful to use common man's terminology when we fight for
> his cause.[17]

Apart from developing local committees and aiding organizational
strength at the grass-roots level, Kanshiram ensured the cultural
re-appropriation of local deities, war heroes, social reformers
and soldiers of the Dalit community.[18] Guru Ravidas, Rani
Jhalkaribai, Uda Devi and others fit into the narrative of politics
that Kanshiram espoused.

Kanshiram's larger objective was the consolidation of the Dalit
vote bank. While he minced no words when he termed some of
his own Dalit brethren 'chamchas' or stooges in the hands of the
upper caste, he did not let his relationship with other Dalit leaders
suffer because of this view of his.[19]

The nation lost Kanshiram on 9 October 2006, after a series
of complications arising from blood pressure, diabetes and a
brain stroke. With his death, a major movement in the history of

post-Independence Dalit politics came to an end. Many important politicians, including the then prime minister, Manmohan Singh, several Congress leaders and even his bête noires Ramvilas Paswan and V.P. Singh paid their respects.

Kanshiram will always be remembered by his slogans. One that especially remains entrenched in the mind and imagination of Dalit activists is '*Jiski jitni sankhya bhari uski utni hissedari*', implying that the road to the equitable distribution of wealth and national resources can only be computed on the basis of representation and numbers.

'I will never get married, I will never acquire any property, I will never visit my home, I will devote and dedicate the rest of my life to achieve the goals of Phule–Ambedkar movement,' Kanshiram used to say.[20] Such was his commitment to public life that he contemporized the learnings of Ambedkar and Phule and was single-handedly able to galvanize the Dalits for concrete political action in pursuit of representation.

In his pragmatic style, Kanshiram sought to restore the lost self-esteem of the Dalits. Until a casteless society was formed, Kanshiram wanted his community to strive to achieve respectable positions in society through political power—and this would be the Dalit war strategy. According to Kanshiram, caste was a double-edged sword that he wanted to use in a way that benefited the Bahujans and destroyed upper-caste hegemony at the same time.[21]

However, there were differences between Ambedkar's and Kanshiram's approaches when it came to this belief. In Kanshiram's own words:

In 1962–63, when I got the opportunity to read Ambedkar's book *Annihilation of Caste*, then I also felt that it is perhaps possible to eradicate casteism from the society. But later on when I studied the caste system and its behaviour in depth, gradually there was a modification in my thoughts. I have not only gained knowledge about caste from the books but from my personal life too. After understanding its functions in Indian society, I have stopped thinking about the annihilation of caste.[22]

An important part of Kanshiram's beliefs was that he mooted the idea of Dalits having their own media, that is, developing a Bahujan media both in English and in Hindi.[23] Another difference was the fact that he learnt from being among the people, from first-hand experiences, from his own life and from the lives of those he met. He said, 'Ambedkar learnt from the books but I have learnt from my own life and people. He used to gather books, I tried to gather people.'[24]

Kanshiram, a democrat at heart, had a vision that was all-inclusive. If Ambedkar framed the Constitution, Kanshiram built a solid political infrastructure for the Dalits to ensure their political empowerment.

A present-day politician who has known and observed Kanshiram from close quarters is Mayawati. He had strong faith in her and groomed her to be the second in command from the very beginning, to one day take over the BSP. Mayawati has aptly summarized his contribution to the Dalit community:

> Manyawar Kanshiram is taller than the tallest peaks of the Himalayas. He is determined to obtain justice for the Bahujan Samaj and he is continuously striving to achieve his goal. There is no limit to his efforts. It is due to his efforts that the Bahujan Samaj is emerging as a new force.[25]

Swami Vivekananda once said,

> Take up one idea. Make that one idea your life—think of it, dream of it, live on that idea. Let the brain, muscles, nerves, every part of your body, be full of that idea, and just leave every

other idea alone. This is the way to success, and this is the way great spiritual giants are produced.[26]

Kanshiram epitomizes this saying in contemporary times. He was not only an original thinker-activist but sincere and passionate about uplifting the Dalits to assert their rights through power, specifically political power, and he channelled all his energy towards that single goal.

Notes

1. A.R. Akela, ed., *Mananiya Behan Kumari Mayawati Ke Saakshatkaar* (Aligarh: Anand Sahitya Sadan, 2008); ANI, 'Kanshi Ram should be given the Bharat Ratna: Mayawati', *DNA*, 15 March 2016, dnaindia. com/india/report-kanshi-ram-should-be-given-the-bharat-ratna-mayawati-2189533.
2. 'Author's note', Badri Narayan, *Kanshiram: Leader of the Dalits*, Penguin Random House India, 2014.
3. 'All You Wanted to Know about Kanshiram', Rediff, 9 October 2016, https://www.rediff.com/news/2006/oct/09kanshi6.htm (accessed on 31 March 20200.
4. Badri Narayan, *Kanshiram: Leader of the Dalits*, Penguin Books India, 2014, p. 11.
5. Ibid, pp. 14–16.
6. Ibid, pp. 19–20.
7. Ibid, p. 21.
8. Ibid, p. 29.
9. Ibid, p. 39.
10. Ibid, p. 41.
11. Ibid, p. 107.
12. Ibid, p. 109.
13. Badri Narayan, *Kanshiram: A Biography*, Penguin Books, p. 113.
14. Ibid, pp. 112–113.
15. 2011 Census of India, Office of the Registrar General and Census Commissioner, Ministry of Home Affairs, Government of India.

16. Kanshiram, *The Chamcha Age: An Era of the Stooges*, Samyak Prakashan, 2018.

17. Ibid, p. 103.

18. Mohan Das Namishray, *Dalit Freedom Fighters*, Gyan Publishing House, 2009, p. 38

19. Kanshiram, *The Chamcha Age*.

20. 'Manyawar Shri Kanshi Ram Ji', Roundtable India for an Informed Ambedkar Age, 12 March 2010, https://roundtableindia.co.in/index.php?option=com_content&view=article&id=1006:manyawar-shri-kanshi-ram-ji&catid=127&Itemid=158 (accessed on 31 March 2020).

21. 'Saheb Kanshi Ram's Speech at First International Dalit Conference', Velivada, 10–11 March 1998, https://velivada.com/2017/10/28/saheb-kanshi-rams-speech-first-international-dalit-conference-kuala-lumpur/ (accessed on 31 March 2020).

22. Badri Narayan, 'Ambedkar and Kanshi Ram: Similar, Yet Different', *Livemint*, 14 October 2009, https://www.livemint.com/Opinion/hXyHXD1PKogjgSs6hI3VxH/Ambedkar-and-Kanshi-Ram-similar-yet-different.html (accessed on 31 March 2020).

23. Badri Narayan, *Kanshiram*, p. 141.

24. Badri Narayan, 'Ambedkar and Kanshi Ram: Similar, Yet Different'.

25. Badri Narayan, *Kanshiram*, p. 1.

26. 'The Complete Works of Swami Vivekananda/Volume 1/Raja-Yoga/Pratyahara And Dharana', Wikipedia, https://en.wikisource.org/wiki/The_Complete_Works_of_Swami_Vivekananda/Volume_1/Raja-Yoga/Pratyahara_And_Dharana (accessed on 31 March 2020).

K.R. Narayanan

Kocheril Raman Narayanan, the first Dalit president of India, was a man of incredible skill. His life's journey is fascinating and can be a great lesson to all of us. Despite being born into a socio-economically backward section of society, he went on to serve as president of the world's largest democracy from 1997 to 2002.

Political commentators have often viewed the office of the president of India as subservient to the real executive in terms of decision-making. In K.R. Narayanan's case, what was most discernible was his commitment to the sacred duty of safeguarding the Constitution of India and spearheading important decisions that enabled the executive class to govern India responsibly within the ambit of parliamentary democracy. He was never a 'yes man' and consistently strove to ensure that the downtrodden, especially the Dalits, were armed with education, and were mainstreamed and recognized. Through this, he ventured beyond the requisite mandate given to the president of India; he was not seen as merely a rubber-stamp head or a symbolic custodian of the Constitution of India.

Narayanan was born on 27 October 1920, in Travancore (present-day Kottayam district, Kerala) the fourth of seven children born to Kocheril Raman Vaidyar and Punnaththuraveettil Paappiyamma. The traditional work of his family, part of the poverty-stricken Paravan caste, was to pick coconuts. However, his father was a respected and learned physician of the traditional Indian medical system of Ayurveda. Vaidyar's vision and foresight were the primary reasons behind the education young Narayanan received. Too poor to buy textbooks, Narayanan was helped in his studies by Neelakantan, his older brother, who would borrow textbooks from others and then copy the notes down for him. Narayanan had to walk 15 kilometres to school every day and paid his fees with the help he received from the Harijan Sevak Sangh, given the lack of reservation in education at the time.[1]

Growing up as a Dalit in Kerala, he was exposed to the brutal realities of caste and social discrimination. In one interview, he admitted that India's parliamentary system could function 'only in an atmosphere of social and economic progress and equality. There had been achievements but the march of society, of social change, has not been fast enough, nor fundamental enough so far.'[2]

For many aspiring politicians, Narayanan symbolizes empowerment through education. He is seen as a person who defied the odds to work towards achieving representation in unseen and unimaginable areas where Dalits were denied their rightful place. Narayanan understood the importance of education in achieving social integration. He believed that change began with the individual.

Narayanan's first published work was written in his school days. He sent an article to the children's section of the popular and credible Malayalam paper, *Malayala Manorama*[3] when in Class IX. In the course of his conversation with Alaka Shankar, who authored his biography *Portrait of a President*, he said,

> I wrote a poem which . . . was edited by the famous writer and humourist E.V. Krishna Pillai of Kerala. However, he did not publish my name at the end of it. He just printed 'A Student'.

I was quite disappointed. And one day in class a letter came addressed to me from E.V. Krishna Pillai. Naturally, my class teacher had to read it first. And the letter stated that he was publishing my poem in the *Manorama Weekly*. The other students were quite surprised. Anyways, that letter was my only proof that I had written that poem.[4]

After completing his school education in his village near the present-day Kottayam district in Kerala, he attained undergraduate and postgraduate degrees in literature from the University of Travancore (now the University of Kerala), with distinction. He was the first Dalit to ever earn a first-class grade in Kerala.[5] Narayanan went to London in 1945 to study political science at the prestigious London School of Economics, thanks to financial assistance from J.R.D. Tata. He was honoured to study under the guidance of renowned scholar, Harold Laski, the famous British political theorist, economist and author. His camaraderie with Laski went on to play a defining role in his political journey.

Narayanan had many stints as a journalist, beginning with *The Hindu* in India and as the London correspondent for *Social Welfare*, a weekly that was run from Mumbai, which was published by K.M. Munshi. In London, he shared a room with K.N. Raj and Veeraswamy Ringadoo, who later became the first president of Mauritius. He was also friends with former prime minister of Canada, Pierre Trudeau.[6]

Narayanan returned to India in 1948 with a letter of introduction from eminent British economist and his teacher at the London School of Economics, Harold Laski, to Jawaharlal Nehru. He soon joined the diplomatic service. Narayanan flourished in the role, going on to become India's ambassador to Thailand, Turkey and China, and and subsequently as a political appointee in the US after his retirement. In 1984, he entered the Parliament with a Congress ticket and, in 1992, was nominated as the vice president of India.

On 16 February 1998, as president of India, Narayanan joined other citizens at a polling booth to cast his vote, which caused an immense furore in the media. That a president was seen with citizens showed how committed he was to his vision, acting in the interest of the common citizenry of the nation.

During his presidential visits to France, leading French dailies such as *Le Figaro*, *Le Monde* and *France Soir* ran headlines such as 'An untouchable in the Elysee palace'.[7] However, Narayanan remained unaffected and focused on the job at hand and his individual journey. He used to say that he was 'not an executive president but a working president, a citizen president working within four corners of the Constitution'.[8] One of his landmark contributions was that he set a new precedent, in which a political leader staking a claim to the prime minister's office produced letters of support from alliance partners that reflected the will of the Parliament.

Narayanan showed us that there are and can exist many ideas of India and that one needed to respect this. At several junctures in his tenure, he spoke about this in detail, of India as a beacon of tolerance. 'India has been a cauldron of dreams, ideas and aspirations of humankind and this is a distinctive character of India, and India in that sense represents the world in miniature. If a system can succeed in India, it will indicate the possibility of such success in the world as a whole.'[9]

Narayanan saw casteism and communalism as two sides of the same coin. When he met Mahatma Gandhi for the first time in Mumbai while he was working for the *Times of India*, he spoke to him about untouchability and how to fight it.

In a speech on the eve of Republic Day in 2001, Narayanan said,

We can show the world that there is room for everybody to live in this country of tolerance and compassion. I have no doubt that through the firmness of our determination and the exercise of our traditional tolerance; India will triumph in the end.[10]

For Narayanan, the Constitution was supreme and safeguarding it was the sacred duty of the office of the president. As a sensitive bureaucrat, he once said, 'Yes-men in public services could be a liability.'[11] He also quoted a well-known Russian saying, 'They say yes and yes until they get you in a mess', as a joke.[12] He once observed that the 'demands of the good bureaucrat (are) an almost superhuman indifference to all his old connections, an almost superhuman capacity to stand apart from the old proclivities of the society around him'.[13]

Narayanan's life urged decision makers and policymakers to absorb Dalits into the mainstream and recognize them, just as he had been supported and recognized as a child and young man. When Narayanan had got his postgraduate degree, it came with recognition and a lot of media attention, and was reported by agencies such as Reuters. At that time, he received a congratulatory letter from Jugal Kishore Birla, scion of the Birla family, and a cheque of Rs 500. These experiences gave Narayanan the affirmation and belief that Indians could recognize and reward anybody who had merit. He urged governments to take social equity seriously.

Social science academics have cited representation of Dalits in sectors such as in the media, politics, industry, judiciary, bureaucracy, universities and civil society as an essential component in contributing to real-time empowerment. In the field of politics, Narayanan is a great example for emulation. The youth in India can take inspiration from the life of Narayanan. As he said, 'My life encapsulates the ability of the democratic system to accommodate and empower marginalised sections of society.'[14] We need this hope in times of despair as well as of resurgence.

Narayanan was honoured with doctorates by many universities across the world. He was once referred to as the 'best diplomat of the country'[15] by Jawaharlal Nehru. The K.R. Narayanan Foundation in Kerala, formed after his death on 9 November 2005, aims to propagate his ideals across the world.

Notes

1. R.A. Mashelkar, 'Dismantling Inequality through Assured Innovation', 19 April 2018 https://mea.gov.in/Portal/CountryNews/9368_KR_NARAYANAN_ORATION.pdf; http://www.millenniumpost.in/sudarshan.ramabadran.and.guru.prakash.

2. 'Shri K.R. Narayanan, President of India: In Conversation with N. Ram on Doordarshan and All India Radio', *The Hindu*, 14 August 1998, https://www.thehindu.com/multimedia/archive/02765/President_K__R__Na_2765855a.pdf (accessed on 31 March 2020).

3. K.M. Mathew, *The Eighth Ring: An Autobiography*, Penguin UK, 2015.

4. Alaka Shankar, *Portrait of a President: K.R. Narayanan*, Children's Book Trust, 2004.

5. 'Remembering K.R. Narayanan with 15 facts on the former President of India', *India Today*, 9 November 2016, https://www.indiatoday.in/education-today/gk-current-affairs/story/k-r-narayanan-349469-2016-11-09 (accessed on 31 March 2020).

6. Vidya Subrahmaniam, 'K.R. Narayanan—President who defied stereotype', *The Hindu*, 10 November 2005, https://www.thehindu.com/2005/11/10/stories/2005111003281400.htm (accessed on 31 March 2020).

7. Rajesh Sharma, 'The Presidential controversy', *Hindu*, 4 June 2000, https://www.thehindu.com/2000/06/04/stories/13040695.htm (accessed on 31 March 2020).

8. Vidya Subrahmaniam, 'K.R. Narayanan—President who defied stereotype', *The Hindu*, 10 November 2005, https://www.thehindu.com/2005/11/10/stories/2005111003281400.htm (accessed on 31 March 2020).

9. 'Shri K.R. Narayanan, President of India: In Conversation with N. Ram on Doordarshan and All India Radio'.

10. K.R Narayanan, 'Address to the Nation on the Eve of Republic Day', presented in New Delhi on 25 January 2001, http://www.krnarayanan.in/html/speeches/others/jan25_2001.htm (accessed on 31 March 2020).

11. K.R. Narayanan, *Images and Insights*, Allied Publishers, 1987.

12. Ibid.

13. Ibid (supra lxxi).

14. 'K.R. Narayanan: Obituary', *The Economist*, 24 November 2005, print edition, https://www.economist.com/obituary/2005/11/24/k.r.-narayanan (accessed on 31 March 2020).

15. Iftikhar Gilani, 'KR Narayanan to RN Kovind—A tale of two Dalit presidents', *DNA*, 20 June 2017, http://www.dnaindia.com/india/report-kr-narayanan-to-rn-kovind-a-tale-of-two-dalit-presidents-2477657 (accessed on 31 March 2020).

Nandanar

Modern-day Tamil Nadu was once the land of some of the greatest rulers of the subcontinent, such as the Cholas, the Cheras and the Pandyas. It has seen some great poets, such as Kamban, Thiruvalluvar and C. Subramania Bharati, and patriots such as Chidambaram Pillai, Subramaniya Shiva and Vanchinathan. It is also considered the home of Bharatanatyam. It was the people from the region now known as Tamil Nadu who, in 1893, persuaded and sent Swami Vivekananda to speak at the World's Parliament of Religions in Chicago.[1] Several social reformers who have enabled reformation by their grit, patience, determination and knowledge have come from here.

These were social reformers who faced the worst and most inexplicable treatment but remained unperturbed. They strove to remain within the ambit of the faith or religion they followed and remove the ills that plagued the minds of the common man in villages. Ambedkar puts it beautifully, 'The Hindus have their social evils. But there is this relieving feature about them, namely that some of them are conscious of their existence, and a few of them are actively agitating for their removal.'[2]

One such saint who stayed within the system and attempted to reform it is Nandanar from Thanjavur in modern-day Tamil Nadu. In fact, he was one of the three SC saints to whom Ambedkar dedicated his book, *The Untouchables*. The *Periya Puranam*, a Tamil account of sixty-three Shaivite saints that was compiled by Sekkizhar in the twelfth century, tells us that Nandanar belonged to Adanur (or Adanoor) in the Chola kingdom (now in Thanjavur). He was born in abject poverty in the Paraiyar caste. People from Nandanar's community were agricultural labourers and singers. An upper-caste member in those days would feel compelled to take a shower if they so much as saw someone from Nandanar's community on the road even from a distance of ten metres.

Nandanar as a labourer was said to have been sincere, hardworking and dedicated. His skills impressed his employers.

The exact dates of the birth and death of Nandanar are not available. It is said that he broke all social barriers with his inner purity. Another depiction of Nandanar's story was made famous by Gopalakrishna Bharati in his *Nandanar Charitram*,[3] a musical in the nineteenth century which was sung in every village in Tamil Nadu.

The story of Nandanar's life was also made into a play and a silent film in 1923 and 1930, respectively. When Tamil cinema began to talk and sing, in 1931, the silent film was produced as a feature film thrice—in 1933, in 1935 and in 1942. The most successful and famous of them all was the last one, in 1942, *Nandanar*, by Gemini Studios.

Popular stories go that when Nandanar went to the Sivaloganatha temple in Tirupunkur, near the famous Vaitheeswaran temple, he could not see the deity as the Nandi blocked his view. His entreaties to the Lord made Shiva instruct Nandi to move aside, allowing Nandanar a clear view of the inner sanctum.[4]

In his pursuit of social integration, Nandanar faced a lot of obstacles and an overall lack of acceptance. His pragmatism was ignored but he stood firm in his pursuit of truth. He was also ridiculed for treading the path of devotion, but he never withered under pressure and remained steadfast in his pursuits. He would grab every opportunity he could to dispel the false beliefs and notions around his community. He sowed vital seeds of social cohesion in them by demonstrating that every individual, irrespective of caste, had the right to God and that all men were created equal. It took a lot of time for him to convince the poverty-stricken, casteism-ridden community of his, but Nandanar did not give up and was devoted to the cause of empowering his community.

Thiruvalluvar, in his magnum opus *Thirukkural*,[5] defined good speaking as being able to hold fast the convinced and being pleasing even to the unconvinced. Nandanar was said to be an orator who appealed to all sensibilities.

There are many myths and legends around Nandanar that are told even now among Dalits. One is of a major obstacle he faced when he desired to visit the Nataraja temple in Chidambaram. Nandanar was duty-bound to approach his master, Vediyar,[6] for permission, who angrily refused him several times, claiming that temples were meant only for the upper castes and that Nandanar did not deserve to go to Chidambaram at all. It is said that the master decided to teach Nandanar a lesson by granting him permission to go on the condition that he would first have to cultivate, reap and harvest forty acres of land!

The story goes that Nandanar was dismayed and shocked to hear of this impossible task. But as a dutiful man who respected orders, he took up the challenge and got to work. He is said to have fainted midway, and legend has it that Nataraja himself miraculously cultivated and kept the entire forty acres of land ready for harvesting overnight. The next morning, Nandanar woke up to see greenery all around him and started singing and dancing in gratitude to the Lord. His master, when he saw the sight the next morning, is said to have realized his mistake and fallen at Nandanar's feet in public view, seeking pardon for his mistake. Nandanar forgave his master and went to Chidambaram in total devotion. When he approached the town, he was thrilled beyond description. However, when he realized that he could not enter the temple owing to his caste, he walked around the town several times and waited in desperate hope that he would see his beloved Nataraja.

It is said that Shiva appeared in the dreams of all upper-caste priests present in the town, asking them to allow Nandanar inside the temple with all due honour. The entire town searched for and identified Nandanar and pleaded with him to enter the temple to get a glimpse of his favourite deity. Even after all this, right when Nandanar was about to set foot inside the temple, a few upper-caste priests objected. They asked him to prove his purity before he was allowed entry. To that effect, they demanded that he jump into a pyre of fire. If he survived, he would be considered pure enough to be allowed entry. Nandanar accepted the task and is said to have surrendered to Shiva.

A pyre was soon built, right outside the temple, and Nandanar is said to have jumped into it by chanting Nataraja's name, and emerged from this with nothing but ash smeared on his body. At this astounding sight, he was taken to the sanctum sanctorum. When Nandanar finally set his eyes on the deity, it is believed that he simply merged into the statue.

The stories of Nandanar remain an inspiration to subaltern communities, especially in their fight for entry into temples, which persists even after seventy-one years of Independence, a true shame and disgrace for the country.

As early as the 1960s, M.S. Golwalkar of the Rashtriya Swayamsevak Sangh (RSS) brought together the heads of various Hindu religious institutions and initiated the passing of a resolution against untouchability. Golwalkar was able to achieve this via the Vishwa Hindu Parishad (VHP) at Udupi in 1966, within a few years of the organization's birth. Saints such as Swami Chinmayananda, who had also been invited to address the World's Parliament of Religions in Chicago, attended this event.

Sanjeev Kelkar, a man highly critical of the RSS and Golwalkar, called this an extraordinary achievement:

> All the Dharmacharyas of the Hindus came together on a level platform. It indicated that all of them had given up (at least outwardly, or on such occasions) their egoistical insistence of their hierarchical privileges, their own sense of high and low among themselves. In one voice they declared that there is no sanction to untouchability in Hindu religion. On this instance, Golwalkar has been described to have been virtually dancing with joy, forgetting the normal restraint and decorum so characteristic of him.[7]

Some temples in India have now made room for SCs and STs to don the role of priests. The RSS magazine, *Panchjanya*, announced in an article in October 2006 that trained individuals from these communities would be appointed as priests in all 'major temples in the country'. The article explained that 'the time has come to strengthen Hindu unity and ensure that along with those priests who are born Brahmins, Dalits and other backward classes are trained and made priests'.[8] In 2008, a priest from an SC community was made the chief priest of the famous Jagannath temple in Bihar.[9] In 2011, Narendra Modi, then the chief minister of Gujarat, asked the Shree Somnath Sanskrit University in Saurashtra to launch a three-year diploma course in priesthood and allocated Rs 22.5 lakh to this initiative. In 2017, Madhya Pradesh launched a similar course.

As a nation, we must strive to live up to the tales and initiatives of Nandanar, to make our country a better place for everyone and ensure that the battle for dignity of the disadvantaged is won by them and for them. Subramania Bharati famously said, 'Tamil Nadu earned sky-high pride by giving Thiruvalluvar to the world.'[10] The same can also be said of Nandanar. Tamil Nadu takes tremendous pride in strong-willed and pure-hearted social reformers such as him.

Notes

1. Sandipan Deb, Vivekananda's 120-year-old 9/11 speech, https://www.livemint.com/Opinion/bCxLFO6mXEnWV5jYzweoII/Vivekanandas-120yearold-911-speech.html

2. B.R. Ambedkar, 'Social Stagnation', *Pakistan Or the Partition of India*, Thackers, 1940.

3. Gopalakrishna Bharathi, *Harikatha Nandanar Charithram*.

4. Sriram V., 'When Nandanar moved the Nandi', *The Hindu*, 19 December 2013, https://www.thehindu.com/features/friday-review/history-and-culture/where-nandanar-moved-the-nandi/article5478475.ece (accessed on 31 March 2020).

5. Thiruvalluvar, *Thirukkural*, Rupa Publications, 2009.

6. A. Kalyanasundaram and Thiru P. Parbhu, *Sivaloganathar Temple at Thirupungur (Tamil Nadu)*, Lulu Publications, 2019, p. 53.

7. Sanjeev Kelkar, *Lost Years of the RSS*, first edition, Sage India, 2011, p. 81.

8. 'RSS for Dalit Head Priests in Temples', *Times of India*, 30 October 2006, https://timesofindia.indiatimes.com/india/RSS-for-Dalit-head-priests-in-temples/articleshow/238039.cms (accessed on 31 March 2020).

9. Aravindan Neelakandan, 'Dalit Priests Are a Welcome Development, but What Did Marxists Have To Do with It?', https://swarajyamag.com/politics/dalit-priests-are-a-welcome-development-but-what-did-marxists-have-to-do-with-it.

10. Sudarshan Ramabadran, 'On Subramania Bharati's death anniversary, remembering India's National Poet', News Minute, 11 September 2017, https://www.thenewsminute.com/article/subramania-bharati-s-death-anniversary-remembering-india-s-national-poet-68234 (accessed on 24 February 2020).

Rani Jhalkaribai

The First War of Independence in 1857 was one of the most important events in Indian history. The names we mostly associate with it are Mangal Pandey, Rani Lakshmibai and Tatya Tope. However, not too many people know of the role Rani Jhalkaribai, also from Jhansi, played in it. In fact, there were several women from the oppressed communities, including Jhalkaribai, Avantibai, Pannadhai, Uda Devi and Mahavirdevi, who deserve mention.[1]

Ambedkar once famously said,

> I am a great believer in woman's organisation. I know what they can do to improve the condition of the society if they are convinced. In the eradication of social evils they have rendered great services. I measure the progress of a community by the degree of progress which women have achieved. Let each girl who marries stand up to her husband, claim to be her husband's friend and equal and refuse to be his slave.[2]

One could read Rani Jhalkaribai's life in light of this statement.

Rani Jhalkaribai was born on 22 November 1830 in Bhojla village near Jhansi as the only daughter of Sadoba Singh and

Jamuna Devi. Her family belonged to the Kori caste. After her mother's death, Jhalkaribai's father raised her to ensure she was trained in the art of weaponry, horse riding and war. While herding cattle in the forest, she is said to have once attacked a leopard with a stick. This story spread to the surrounding villages and made her a popular figure.[3] Koris, also known as Kolis, claim descent from Kabir, who, during his lifetime, questioned and challenged orthodoxy within the religious order. The president of India, Ram Nath Kovind, also from the Kori caste, unveiled a statue of Jhalkaribai at Guru Tegh Bahadur Complex in Bhopal on 10 November 2017.

If there is one warrior who epitomized renowned Chinese military strategist Sun Tzu's striking quote 'Attack is the secret of defence; defence is the planning of an attack',[4] it was Rani Jhalkaribai. Legend has it that her husband, Puran Koree of Namampur in Jhansi, played a key role in honing her battle skills by training her in archery, wrestling and shooting.[5]

It is also said that in her complexion and physical stature, Jhalkaribai bore a striking resemblance to Lakshmibai. This is documented in an account written by B.L. Varma in 1951, in which he interviews Jhalkaribai's grandson. He underlines that she was a trusted adviser of Rani Lakshmibai and not her domestic help.[6] According to Varma, Jhalkaribai was included in the women's army banded together by Lakshmibai, and she learnt her skills in archery, wrestling and shooting from the latter. Jhalkaribai inspired her husband, Puran Koree, to fight for Lakshmibai.[7]

Bundelkhand, where Rani Jhalkaribai lived at one point, is home to another important legend. Her prowess in battles is believed to have stunned the British generals. As one went on to say, 'Even if one per cent of Indian women were like Jhalkari, the British would soon have to leave India.'[8] Another famous saying goes, '*Macha Jhansi mein ghamasan, chahun aur machee kilkari thee, Angrezon se loha lenein, ran mein kudee Jhalkari thee*', which means

'Amidst the sound and fury of the battle at Jhansi, Jhalkari plunged herself into the battlefield to confront the British.'[9]

Jhalkaribai was a shrewd strategist and became one of the most trusted advisers of Rani Lakshmibai. She was always battle-ready and at the forefront to develop strategies to protect the queen. There was one strategy in particular that worked well during the rebellion. Under the infamous Doctrine of Lapse, the British were looking to take over the kingdom of Jhansi and the Gwalior fort, but Lakshmibai would not budge. It was then, when battle raged at the gates of the fort, that Jhalkaribai disguised herself as the queen and fought from the frontline as a ploy to let Lakshmibai escape the fort, which was almost under siege.[10]

In the words of Raj Kumar Koree, a singer in the Jababi Kirtan Mandali, '*U to Durga rahin*' (She was goddess Durga).[11] Jababi Kirtan is a popular cultural performance in the Bundelkhand region and the stories and deeds of Jhalkaribai are a common subject in most Kirtan mandals (devotional song groups)[12] and part of popular culture in the region. Her legacy has survived in people's memory and is often reaffirmed through folklores, folk stories and discussions at village squares.[13]

However, beyond oral history, Jhalkaribai remains largely unknown. Such is this negligence that she is not even part of school curriculums today. A novel in 1951 by Ram Chandra Heran, titled *Maati*, gives students of history but a glimpse of Jhalkaribai. The first biography to ever have been written on her was in 1964 by Bhawani Shankar Visharad, an account inspired by Varma's book. Visharad's book includes popular stories narrated by people of the Bundelkhand region on Jhalkaribai. Apart from the oral legacy, her stories have also been immortalized in cultural performances such as dramas. In 1990, Mata Prasad, then governor of Arunachal Pradesh, wrote a drama on her called *Jhalkaribai Natak*.[14]

Other fascinating ways of remembering Jhalkaribai have been the annual commemoration of her legend at the fort of Lakshmi in Jhansi, a tower near Unnao Gate and Anjani Toria named after her and a polytechnic college instituted by Dalits in Jhansi in her memory. There is also a Veerangana Memorial Trust to help the transmission of the story of Jhalkaribai.[15]

There's now a statue of Jhalkaribai in Jhansi, thanks to the then Mayawati government. The BSP has been at the forefront of reinstating Jhalkaribai in the annals of history and in public memory through its outreach and campaign activities. In fact, the Bundelkhand region has the maximum number of Dalit population (80.6 per cent)[16] in Uttar Pradesh; Mayawati's BSP secured over 47 per cent votes in the 1996 state elections. One of the factors said to contribute to the party's fortunes is the bringing back of Jhalkaribai into public memory.[17] The BSP has been organizing festivals centred on her in every village block as well.[18]

The deep-seated patriarchy and intellectual feudalism that one sees in Indian academia need to end. The aim is to not remain divided as a community but united by taking inspiration from individuals such as Jhalkaribai.

In 2001, the Government of India under Prime Minister Atal Bihari Vajpayee released a stamp in honour of Rani Jhalkaribai. In the description that accompanied the stamp release, the government said, 'She is a living memory in the folklore of the Bundelkhand region (which was part of the erstwhile state of Jhansi) even today. Jhalkari was a village girl who had to take charge of the household chores in her childhood itself, following the early loss of her mother.'[19]

Today Dalits are viewed mainly as a political commodity.[20] This perception must change to ensure that the community is not only viewed as political but also social and intellectual capital. Bringing icons such as Rani Jhalkaribai back into the mainstream political narrative can be a start.

While it would be prudent to introduce her into history textbooks, strong policy interventions towards empowering the disadvantaged will also serve Rani Jhalkaribai's memory. In 2005, as part of a special report[21] on the status of the SCs, which the National Commission of Schedule Castes submitted to the Central government in 2005, Suraj Bhan, as chairman, suggested a small amendment to Article 17 of the Constitution. According to him, instead of the article stating 'Untouchability is abolished and its practice in any form is forbidden', it should read, 'Caste system and untouchability stand abolished.' Historically, Bhan's recommendation was a continuation of Ambedkar's vision to bring an end to this social evil. In his book *Annihilation of Caste*, he states:

> Caste is a notion. It is a state of the mind. The destruction of Caste does not therefore mean the destruction of a physical barrier. It means a notional change. People are not wrong in observing Caste. In my view, what is wrong is their religion, which has inculcated this notion of Caste. If this is correct, then obviously the enemy you must grapple with is not the people who observe Caste, but the Shastras which teach them this religion of Caste. Criticising and ridiculing people for not inter-dining or inter-marrying or occasionally holding inter-caste dinners and celebrating inter-caste marriages, is a futile method of achieving the desired end. The real remedy is to destroy the belief in the sanctity of the Shastras. How do you expect to succeed, if you allow the Shastras to continue to mould the beliefs and opinions of the people?[22]

While some stringent policy interventions to bridge social inequalities have to be made, the issue must also be tackled at the individual level. Unless brute, uncomfortable questions are part of our everyday conversations, it will be difficult to carry forward the legacy of Rani Jhalkaribai or contribute to social integration. Some important questions to ask are:

• Have the citizens of India made a conscious attempt to integrate and remember Dalit icons as part of this country?

- Do we realize that the right to equality, regardless of caste and gender, is a fundamental one?
- Do we question it when basic rights are denied to a particular community? Do we ask what we, as responsible citizens, can do to address these differences?

Unless such questions and conversations feature in our day-to-day lives, India will not win the battle in ensuring that Dalits are represented in every sphere of life, equally and amicably. It takes tremendous strength and courage to fight the wrongs done in society, but we have inspiration in the form of many individuals such as Rani Jhalkaribai who have led the way.

Notes

1. Mohan Das Namishray, *Dalit Freedom Fighters*, Gyan Publishing House, 2009, p. 20.
2. Bhalchandra Mungekar, ed., *The Essential Ambedkar*, Rupa Publications, 2017, pp. 383–84.
3. Nupur Preeti Alok, 'Jhalkari Bai: The Indian Rebellion of 1857 and Forgotten Dalit History', Feminism India, 22 November 2016, https://feminisminindia.com/2016/11/22/jhalkari-bai-dalit-woman-essay/ (accessed on 11 January 2020).
4. Sun Tzu, *The Art of War*, first edition, Jaico Publishing House, 2010.
5. Alok, 'Jhalkari Bai'.
6. Das Namishray, *Dalit Freedom Fighters*, p. 24.
7. Ibid, p. 25.
8. Shrikishan Saral, *Indian Revolutionaries: A Comprehensive Study, 1757-1961*, vol. 1, Ocean Books, 1999, p. 113.
9. Badri Narayan, *Women Heroes and Dalit Assertion in North India: Culture, Identity and Politics*, Sage, 2006, p. 122.
10. Das Namishray, *Dalit Freedom Fighters*, p. 25.
11. Ibid, p. 23.
12. Ibid.
13. Ibid.
14. Ibid, p. 25.

15. Ibid, p. 27.
16. Narayan, *Women Heroes and Dalit Assertion in North India: India'*, p. 130.
17. Ibid, p. 131.
18. Ibid, p. 127.
19. Guru Prakash and Sudarshan Ramabadran, 'Denying Dalits their place in history: Time to awaken Rani Jhalkaribai to India', News Minute, 26 November 2016, https://www.thenewsminute.com/article/denying-dalits-their-place-history-time-awaken-rani-jhalkaribai-india-53461 (accessed on 31 March 2020).
20. 'Dalit BJP leader Sanjay Paswan attacks party over "tokenism"', *Economic Times*, 15 June 2016, https://economictimes.indiatimes.com/news/politics-and-nation/dalit-bjp-leader-sanjay-paswan-attacks-party-over-tokenism/articleshow/52762932.cms?from=mdr (accessed on 31 March 2020).
21. Anuradha Raman, 'Abolish Caste', *Outlook*, 31 October 2005, https://www.outlookindia.com/magazine/story/abolish-caste/229095 (accessed on 31 March 2020).
22. B.R. Ambedkar, with an introduction by Arundhati Roy, *Annihilation of Caste: The Annotated Critical Edition*, Navayana, 2014.

Jogendranath Mandal

A lesser-known and underrated personality who fought for and asserted the rights of Dalits in India till his very last breath is Jogendranath Mandal. Time and again, his loyalty to India has been questioned because of his life story—that in his political career, he chose to work in cohesion with the Muslim League and Mohammad Ali Jinnah, and as a result pledged allegiance to Pakistan, only to be later disillusioned about his choice. He remains a forgotten leader, despite being multidimensional in his political skills, all because he chose to shift to Pakistan as law minister.

Whether it was in education, the judiciary, the economy, politics or even cooperative bodies, Mandal always stood for adequate representation of Dalits and gave voice to their concerns and oppressions in any form he could. It is unfortunate that his name skips mention in the biographies of India, Pakistan and Bangladesh.[1] Perhaps he was the only Dalit leader to serve as a minister in the last two governments of undivided Bengal (1943–46) and the first government of Pakistan (1947–50).[2]

Mandal was born in a Namasudra (largest lower caste of Bengal, formerly called Chandal) family on 29 January 1904, in the Maisterkandi village of the Barisal district in what was then the Bengal Presidency under British India—today's Bangladesh. He was the youngest of six children, born to Ramdayal Mandal and Sandhyadebi. He passed his BA examinations in 1932 from B.M. College in Barisal. He then joined the Calcutta Law College and passed the law examination in 1934.[3] Beyond this not much is known of Jogendranath Mandal's early years.

Mandal, who was deeply influenced by Netaji Subhas Chandra Bose and Sarat Chandra Bose, began his political career as an independent candidate in the Indian provincial assembly elections of 1937 by winning a general seat. He contested from Bakharganj North East Rural Constituency for a seat in the Bengal Legislative Assembly and defeated Saral Kumar Dutta, the president of the district committee of the Indian National Congress (INC).

Despite Mahatma Gandhi's efforts to reach out to Jogendranath Mandal to join the INC, Mandal didn't, as he found the Congress casteist.[4] Instead, he worked to bring together the All Bengal Scheduled Castes Federation and the Calcutta Scheduled Caste League to ensure adequate representation of SCs in the legislature. It is at this stage that Mandal even proposed the reorganization of the Independent Scheduled Castes Assembly party.[5]

However, subsequently, in 1940, since Mandal was close to both the Bose brothers, he contested on a reserved seat as a Congress candidate in the Calcutta Municipal Corporation in 1940 and won.[6] In 1943, he extended support to the Nazimuddin government in Bengal and became a minister to lead key portfolios such as Co-operative Credit and Rural Indebtedness.[7]

Another interesting fact about Mandal's close bond with Netaji is that after Netaji was removed from the INC, Mandal began his tryst with the Muslim League.[8] Subsequently, after Netaji formed the Forward Bloc, Mandal accompanied him on a tour when the former visited Barisal. Bose respected Mandal because of his 'honeyed behaviour, unwavering determination and his singular devotion to service', embracing him like one would a brother.[9]

Ambedkar and Mandal's friendship deserves mention as well. When Ambedkar established the All India Scheduled Caste Federation (AISCF), he deputed Mandal to head the Bengal Scheduled Caste Federation (BSCF).[10] In the general election of 1946 that followed, Mandal stood on a BSCF ticket and won. He was straightaway inducted into the legislative ministry under H.S. Suhrawardy.[11]

Mandal played a vital role in the framing of the Constitution as well. There were occasions when Ambedkar sought his advice through letters on matters pertaining to the framing of the Constitution.[12] Beyond this, not much is available on the specific contributions he made.

It is relevant to note here that Mandal was instrumental in Ambedkar's getting elected to the Constituent Assembly, thereby facilitating his political career. It was around this time that Mandal and Ambedkar established the Bengal branch of the Scheduled Castes Federation (SCF). Ambedkar failed to win the Bombay Provincial Assembly election in 1946, but Mandal ensured he rallied enough support for Ambedkar to enter the Constituent Assembly.[13]

In 1946, the British government proposed election of the members to the Constituent Assembly of India by members of the Provincial Assemblies. For this Ambedkar came to Calcutta (now Kolkata) to seek support from the European members of the Bengal Legislative Assembly. But the latter decided not to participate in the elections. It was then that Mandal began to rally people around to vote for Ambedkar in Bengal. With Mandal's efforts and reassurance, Ambedkar was elected from the state with the highest number of votes in Bengal.[14] The Congress opposed Ambedkar's contesting of elections, so it can be said that it was mainly because of Mandal that we had one of the finest minds in India working on our Constitution.

Although Ambedkar's fight was against both the Congress and the Muslim League, he reaffirmed his support for Mandal, even when he was made the first law minister of Pakistan by Jinnah. Ambedkar saw Mandal's elevation in Pakistan as a clever strategy by Jinnah to signal that even Indians were in favour of Partition, but never stopped Mandal from taking on the responsibility.[15] In their friendship, one can discern a mutual admiration bound by the cause both of them were serving, that is Dalit-led empowerment.

Mandal used political power to reaffirm his stand in ensuring adequate representation for Dalits. As part of the Bengal Legislative Assembly, Mandal made several key arguments in their favour. He called for the representation of Dalits in key roles in the cooperative department of Barisal and in the posts of debt settlement officers.[16]

One of Mandal's debut interventions in the Bengal Assembly was on the amendments proposed during the discussions on the Bengal Tenancy Bill and, given his legal background, he posed questions to the judicial and legislative departments about the number of suits for the enhancement of rent in different courts of the Sadar subdivision of Bakarganj.[17]

He was also committed to providing quality education for Dalits—he tried to change the Bhegai Halder Public Academy in Agailjhara, a secondary school at the time, to a higher-secondary one. Along with helping raise funds for the school, he also spread awareness on the importance of education. Mandal got government assistance for this with help from Syama Prasad Mookerjee, a towering figure in Bengal politics at the time.[18]

History tells us that it was Ambedkar who espoused the cause of reservation for Dalits, but even before him, Mandal encouraged the idea as he felt that through reservation, representation would be guaranteed for the Dalits. This is evident in his rationale behind working with the Muslim League in Pakistan, in which he sought the inclusion of SC ministers in the Cabinet as well as an annual monetary grant for the education and representation of the SCs in government services.[19]

On 5 August 1947, Mandal left for Karachi to join the Pakistan government. He was elected as their first law and labour minister and was the only high-ranking Hindu member of the government. In each of his interventions in the Pakistan Constituent Assembly, Mandal spoke on behalf of the Hindus and the SCs in Pakistan.[20]

But on 8 October 1950, Mandal migrated to West Bengal after resigning from his ministerial position in the Pakistani Cabinet as a mark of protest against the continuous repression of the Hindu minorities in East Pakistan. His long 8013-word letter of resignation[21] makes it clear that when he left Pakistan, he felt a deep frustration in the way the subaltern community, especially the Dalit Hindus, were being treated.[22]

In the letter, he minced no words when he proudly stated that he stood for the cause of the deprived Hindus. As a minister in Pakistan, he was constantly sceptical and opposed the Objectives Resolution passed in 1949. Mandal questioned Pakistan on its deteriorating state when it came to Hindus, especially Dalit Hindus. He said in his resignation letter, 'Pakistan is no place for Hindus to live in.' He went on to say, 'Hindus of Pakistan have to all intents and purposes been rendered "stateless" in their own houses.'[23]

Mandal and Ambedkar were both against the Partition. They both held the firm view that it would not better the situation of the Muslims, and Mandal even forewarned that as a result of the Partition, Pakistan would be one of the most underdeveloped countries in Southeast Asia.[24]

When the Muslim League called for Direct Action Day reinforcing the demand for a separate Muslim country called Pakistan on 16 August 1946, Mandal visited several parts of East Bengal and called for peace and calm. He also wrote an article in the Bengali journal *Jagaran* asking subaltern readers to exercise restraint.[25]

Mandal expressed his displeasure with then prime minister Liaquat Ali Khan. According to Mandal, Pakistan continued to pursue a policy that was not just anti-Hindu but against the disadvantaged sections of society; despite his best efforts, he saw no change in the situation and was left with no option but to detail in his resignation letter the brutality unleashed on Dalit Hindus in Pakistan.[26] He emphasized how Dalits were lured by the Muslim League's politics, which later proved disastrous for them. This is precisely why Mandal's realization that he may have made the wrong choice is a great lesson. In fact, Pakistani poet Akhtar Baloch wrote of him: 'You have died for them, but they won't bother to attend your funeral.'[27]

The situation in East Bengal reflected the shame, boycott and disgrace that the Hindus faced, especially the Dalits. Through Mandal's sensational resignation letter, one can feel the pain faced by Dalits in Pakistan. In the letter he unequivocally stated that Dalits were being forcibly converted to Islam or killed. Those who could manage to migrate to India from Pakistan were doing so.[28]

Mandal dedicated his life to enabling the empowerment of Hindus. On seeing the horrific treatment meted out to Hindu minorities in Pakistan, he knew his conscience would not permit him to continue in office in Pakistan's Central government. He did not want to create any false impression in the minds of Pakistani Hindus or those abroad that Hindus could live there with honour, respect and a a sense of security.[29]

In 1950, when Mandal returned to India, he dived into work and began the rehabilitation of refugees who had migrated from East Pakistan. To this end, he also took out several demonstrations that these refugees not be shifted out of West Bengal. He joined hands with a cross-political party organization United Central Refugee Council, that included members from the Communist Party of India (CPI) but later parted ways due to ideological differences, and soon after founded the Eastern India Refugee Council.[30]

Though he could not secure victory in politics in India, he tried to make a mark through the Republican Party of India in 1967,[31] but unfortunately failed at the attempt. Mandal died on 5 October 1968 at the age of sixty-four, in Bangaon, West Bengal. It is said that he died while conducting an election campaign at the site of one of West Bengal's largest refugee camps.[32]

In West Bengal, Mandal was committed to serving as many refugees as he could who were migrating from Pakistan—he was never short-sighted in measure. He empathized with their pain and agony. Mandal's contribution, his life, his vision and his mission are today hardly remembered by Indian historians and leaders. Mandal stood for 'empowerment', not 'entitlement'. Just like what the Dalit youth want today, Mandal wanted people from disadvantaged communities to engage in and explore the larger world that was denied to them.

Today, there are several schools and colleges named after Mandal in West Bengal. North 24 Parganas also organizes annual meetings on his birth and death anniversaries. Today, the Dalit discourse in India needs optimism, and no one epitomizes it better than Mandal. He stood for social equity as well as representation of the Dalits in mainstream society. In pursuit of political power, his demands were clear—that his community advance and empower itself by seeking representation in various quarters. There is also no denying the fact that he was critical of both the Congress and the Hindu Mahasabha for their feeble attempts to resolve the caste question.[33]

There has been and continues to be a lot of discussion around why he left India for Pakistan. But no matter where he was, he didn't, for once, give up championing the rights of the disadvantaged or the weak. To many, including us, he remains a champion of Bengal's underprivileged, a person who always lived on his own terms and a leader who stood for the political and economic equality of the subaltern.

Notes

1. Debashis Sarkar, 'Jogendranath Mandal: A Forgotten Political Leader of Bengal', *MS Academic*, October 2017, vol. 7, no. 2, pp. 17–22.
2. Ibid.
3. '29th January in Dalit History – Birth anniversary of Jogendranath Mandal', Dr B.R. Ambedkar's Caravan, 29 January 2015, https://drambedkarbooks.com/2015/01/29/29th-january-in-dalit-history-birth-anniversary-of-jogendranath-mandal/#more-2751 (accessed on 31 March 2020).
4. Dwaipayan Sen, 'Representation, Education and Agrarian Reform: Jogendranath Mandal and the Nature of Schedule Caste Politics, 1937-1943', *Modern Asian Studies*, vol. 48, no. 1.
5. 'Scheduled Castes Federation dissatisfied with work of present ministry', *Hindusthan Standard*, 27 July 1938, Jagadishchandra Mandal, *Mahapran Jogendranath, Pratham Khanda*, pp. 48–9. The meeting was held at the residence of Guruprasad Das, a former member of the legislative council, and was attended by the following MLAs: Hem Chandra Naskar, Rasiklal Biswas, Kshetra Mohan Singha, Pushpajit Barman, Jogendranath Mandal and others.
6. Sarkar, 'Jogendranath Mandal'.
7. Ibid.
8. Arnav Das Sharma, 'Selective Memory', *Caravan*, 1 April 2017, https://caravanmagazine.in/perspectives/jogendra-nath-mandal-bjp-bsp-up-election-2017 (accessed 31 March 2020).
9. Sen, 'Representation, Education and Agrarian 'Reform'.
10. Sarkar, 'Jogendranath Mandal'.
11. Ibid.
12. 'Ambedkar's letter to Jogendranath Mandal', YouTube, 1 November 2013, https://www.youtube.com/watch?v=SW6x8LzDa38 (accessed on 31 March 2020).
13. S.N.M. Abdi, 'Attention BJP: When the Muslim League rescued Ambedkar from the "dustbin of history"', Firstpost, 15 April 2015, https://www.firstpost.com/india/attention-sanghis-when-the-muslim-league-rescued-ambedkar-from-the-dustbin-of-history-2196678.html

14. Salim Yusufji, *Ambedkar: The Attendant Details*, Navayana, first edition, 2017, p. 91.
15. Ibid, p. 96.
16. Sen, 'Representation, Education and Agrarian Reform'.
17. Ibid.
18. Ibid.
19. Appendix 1, 'Jogendra Nath Mandal's Resignation Letter to Liaquat Ali Khan'.
20. Sarkar, 'Jogendranath Mandal'.
21. Sunanda K. Datta Ray, 'A Different Tragedy', *Telegraph*, 6 June 2015, https://www.telegraphindia.com/opinion/a-different-tragedy/cid/1441069 (accessed on 31 March 2020).
22. Sarkar, 'Jogendranath Mandal'.
23. Appendix 1, 'Jogendra Nath Mandal's Resignation Letter to Liaquat Ali Khan'.
24. Ibid.
25. Das Sharma, 'Selective Memory'.
26. Appendix 1, 'Jogendra Nath Mandal's Resignation Letter to Liaquat Ali Khan'.
27. Ashutosh Bhardwaj, 'Eye on Uttar Pradesh polls, BJP showcases Pakistan Dalit minister who "came back disillusioned"', *Indian Express*, 28 June 2016, https://indianexpress.com/article/india/india-news-india/uttar-prdesh-assembly-election-bjp-dalit-votes-jogendra-nath-mandal-amit-shah-2880221/ (accessed on 31 March 2020).
28. Appendix 1, 'Jogendra Nath Mandal's Resignation Letter to Liaquat Ali Khan'.
29. Ibid.
30. Sarkar, 'Jogendranath Mandal'.
31. Sen, 'Representation, Education and Agrarian Reform'.
32. Sarkar, 'Jogendranath Mandal'.
33. Sen, 'Representation, Education and Agrarian Reform'.

Valmiki

'We are not makers of history, we are made by history,' said the legendary Martin Luther King Jr.[1] If we go back to the Indic civilizational past, Sage Valmiki, one of India's greatest poets due to his sheer intellectual brilliance, epitomized this very quote. His work has caught the attention of not just Indian scholars but those in Southeast Asia and Western countries as well. Valmiki and his works are an important subject of study. Born Ratnakar, he is considered the *adikavi*, or the first poet, of India.[2] It is said that Valmiki composed his first poem out of sorrow when he saw a male bird shot down by a hunter and its mate crying.[3]

But what turned Ratnakar into Valmiki? What is it that stands out about him that leaves in all his admirers a deep sense of commitment to change?

His life is shrouded in mystery. All that any biographer can do is read up on traditions that refer to Valmiki, sift thorugh the information and study the evolution of his life.[4] While the importance of the author of the Ramayana remains indisputable, we are only able to make biographical sense of this Hindu legend through the past.[5]

One of the most popular and contested legends around Valmiki is that of his transformation to being a poet sage, thanks to his meeting with Sage Narada. As the story goes, Ratnakar, a waylayer raised by hunters,[6] happened to meet Sage Narada on a cold, dark night, when he intended to steal from him in a deserted forest. Narada was said to bring social change and spiritual growth wherever he went, employing ways to bring people closer to God. When Ratnakar waylaid him, Narada convinced the former to ask his family whether they would partake in his sins. Ratnakar, upon hearing their responses in the negative, apologized to Narada and begged him to show the path of atonement. On Narada's advice, he began to chant Rama's name with such devotion that he remained oblivious to an ant hill that formed around him. When Narada returned and saw this, he cleared the ant hill and named Ratnakar 'Valmiki', meaning ant hill.[7] He convinced Ratnakar to chant 'Mara, Mara', 'Rama, Rama' in reverse. As per this legend, it is believed that this simple practice transformed and set Valmiki on the path of social transformation and spiritual change.[8] Valmiki's intense meditation spoke of his singleminded focus and purity of intention. It was perhaps his devotion and dedication to chanting the name of Rama that he could write the Ramayana.[9] The text, rich in literary and poetic excellence, is considered one of the greatest literary works in the world. Valmiki's Ramayana is considered the oldest among the many versions of the Ramayana.

Ramayana is considered as *itihasa*, placing it in the category of history and not myth, which means it documents true events. However, this does not mean everything mentioned in the Ramayana happened just as they appear in the text—in the process of telling and retelling, embellishments are inevitable.[10]

In his dialogue with Narada, Valmiki is said to have asked the wandering sage whether he knew any man who was truly virtuous, mighty, righteous, truthful, steadfast in his vows, of exemplary conduct, benevolent to all creatures, learned, capable, good-looking, self-controlled, of proper temperament, judicious, envy-free and fearsome in battle. Narada answered that so many qualities, though hard to find in one person, Rama, born in the Ikshvaku lineage, was known among the people as one such person ('*ikṣvākuvaṃśa prabhavo rāmo nāma janaiḥ śrutaḥ*', or 'Rama, born in the Ikṣhvaku lineage, is known among the people as one such person).[11]

There is yet another story that talks about what inspired Valmiki to write the Ramayana. It is said that when he had gone with his disciple Bharadvaja to bathe in the waters of River Tamasa, he saw a pair of curlews in the act of making love. However, the male bird was shot by a hunter and killed. As the female grieved, Valmiki was moved by this scene and, driven by compassion, uttered his very first shloka. Since it was composed in an act of sorrow (*shoka*), this kind of composition came to be known as the shloka. Unknowingly, he had uttered the first verse in Sanskrit literature, and was adorned as the adikavi, or the first poet. Later, Brahma, the creator of the world, heard these words and urged Valmiki to write the Ramayana.[12]

The Ramayana is considered the pillar of Indic civilization, an integral part of Indian psyche, worship and everyday life. It has more than 24,000 verses, divided into seven cantos—Balakanda, Ayodhyakanda, Aranyakanda, Kishkindakanda, Sundarakanda, Yuddhakanda and Uttarakanda. Valmiki's Ramayana is the *adi kavya*, the source from which all other Ramayanas draw their inspiration. Following Sage Valmiki's Ramayana, the king poet Kamban composed *Ramavataram* in Tamil; Goswami Tulsidas composed *Ramacharitamanas* in the Avadhi language; the poet Kalidas also included the story of Rama in his famous composition, *Raghu Vamsha*, in Sanskrit. Taking the thread of stories from Valmiki's, many other poets have also composed smaller poems, stories, dramas and other texts around the Ramayana. Translations and commentaries on Valmiki's Ramayana continue even today, keeping its legacy alive.

It would be naive to confine the popularity of the Ramayana to modern Indian borders. It is read and performed in various countries, including Indonesia, Singapore, Cambodia, Thailand and Malaysia. The epic is not only a reflection of the strong cultural and civilizational links India has with these countries but is also a binding factor. In January 2018, to commemorate twenty-five years of India-ASEAN (Association for South East Asian Nations) relations, India organized a Ramayana festival as part of the celebrations.

Some scholars have described Valmiki as Rama's contemporary.[13] Through the Ramayana, Valmiki tells us that if one looks around the world, the man who comes closest to the ideal human being is Rama. The Ramayana is his story—his journey through life and how he deals with its vicissitudes, how he tries to maintain the ideal and how he remains ethical in the face of adversity and tragedy. However, Rama is culpable in questioning his wife's purity and thereby losing her, but Rama as a king and a person is an ideal to strive for.

Indian freedom fighter and spiritual stalwart Sri Aurobindo expounds the Ramayana as embodying the roots of Indian culture. In an essay he beautifully talks about the significance of the Ramayana as a potent force of intellectual conception and living presentation:

> The Ramayana . . . is less of the philosophic, more of the purely poetic mind, more of the artist, less of the builder. The whole story is from beginning to end of one piece and there is no deviation from the stream of the narrative . . . The work of Valmiki has been an agent of almost incalculable power in the moulding of the cultural mind of India: it has presented to it to be loved and imitated in figures like Rama and Sita, made so divinely and with such a revelation of reality as to become objects of enduring cult and worship, or like Hanuman, Lakshmana, Bharata the living human image of its ethical

ideals; it has fashioned much of what is best and sweetest in the national character, and it has evoked and fixed in it those finer and exquisite yet firm soul tones and that more delicate humanity of temperament which are a more valuable thing than the formal outsides of virtue and conduct.[14]

Through the Ramayana we also get a glimpse of Valmiki's life. The second chapter of the epic reveals that Valmiki is an articulate and persuasive speaker, along with being a virtuous and intelligent man who had a following of his own.[15] He is described as a 'great souled . . . dvija' or a 'twice-born rsi',[16] in the epics.[17] The third and fourth chapters of the Ramayana describe Valmiki as 'saintly' and 'holy', drawing the picture of an extraordinary individual—'muni, rsi, ascetic; high-minded, innately wise, trained in religious ritual, and learned in matters of dharma worthy of the company of the Gods'.[18] It is at this point in the Ramayana that he is bestowed with spiritual vision, attained through meditation and not recitation, of the poetic story of Prince Rama, told eloquently in the epic through some 24,000 shloka verses.[19] The issue with these rich descriptions is, however, the lack of information regarding Valmiki's early life.

There are multiple legends and stories around Valmiki's social origin. According to R.C. Bulcke, Valmiki taught his composition to the kuśīlavas. Unlike the *sūta* bards (who were usually royal eulogists), the *kuśīlavas* (wandering balladists), who hailed from a lower caste, had a very low status in society. Bulcke leaves the aspect of Valmiki's social origin inconclusive by posing a question to his readers that since Valmiki's disciples are wandering balladists, is it possible or probable that Valmiki himself may have been one? He then goes on to say that by the time the Ramayana was composed, Valmiki was a legendary ascetic.[20]

In addition to the Ramayana, another fascinating book attributed to Valmiki is *Yoga Vasishtha*, which epitomizes Advaita Vedanta. This book is also the source of many philosophical discussions that one finds cited in texts of later periods, such as Swami Vidyaranya's *Jivanmuktiviveka*.[21] Although this book has inspired great scholars and thinkers such as Shankaracharya, Madhvacharya and Narayana Bhatta, it has not achieved the popularity of the Bhagavad Gita and the Upanishads.[22] About the greatness of *Yoga Vasishtha*, Valmiki, its author, is quite eloquent himself. At several places in the text, he says that as far as self-knowledge is concerned, there is no scripture better than it.[23] One of the most defining aspects of *Yoga Vasishtha* is that it does not limit itself—it speaks of how women can attain moksha and also teach others how to acquire it. In fact, it talks about how even animals, such as serpents and crows, can be liberated from the cycle of life and death.[24]

Valmiki's writings, especially his descriptions of nature, are lyrical and superlative, similar to Kalidasa's. Some scholars believe the Ramayana was composed between 2350 BC and 1500 BC, and some others place it at 3000 BC.[25] Yet others choose to stay away from mentioning a time frame.[26] Scholars have estimated that Valmiki's *Yoga Vasishta* was composed in its present form between the sixth and the fourteenth centuries.[27]

As far as the Ramayana is concerned, even though not much is known about its author apart from legends and fables that have been passed down, no one can argue against its literary merit. Was it because he was a Dalit that there is so little of him documented in history or was it a conscious decision taken by Valmiki himself? While there is no answer to this, a choice can be made now to include him in the list of eminent Dalit personalities who transcended the additional social barriers that were a result of the castes they were born into.

Valmiki Jayanti, the birth anniversary of Valmiki, is also referred to as Pragat Diwas.[28] It is celebrated on the full-moon day during the month of Ashwin, which corresponds to the months of September–October in the Gregorian calendar. India is home to several Valmiki temples, but the most prominent one is perhaps the one in Thiruvanmiyur, Chennai. It is believed to be around 1,300 years old and stands on the East Coast Road in the aptly named Valmiki Nagar. Legend has it that after writing the Ramayana, Valmiki rested at the spot where the temple now stands. The Valmiki temple is now under the supervision of the prominent Marundeeswarar temple, which was constructed during the Chola reign. It is believed that Sage Valmiki visited the Marundeeswarar temple to worship Lord Shiva, following which the region was named Thiruvalmikiyur and then later Thiruvanmiyur.[29]

There is today a Valmiki community that worships the poet as its ancestor and god, and marks Valmiki Jayanti with a grand procession. The members constitute about 16 per cent of India's population, numbering nearly 15 lakh in Uttar Pradesh alone. The community can also be found in Haryana, Punjab, Delhi, Gujarat and Chandigarh, where they are locally known by other names. Sadly, they are all socially excluded. Valmikis are employed as sweepers in municipalities, hospitals and government offices. Some are engaged in agricultural or contract labour. They are also into ancillary occupations such as pig rearing, basket weaving and poultry farming. Some from the community, such as the Mehtars of Bihar, play drums at weddings and festivals while the womenfolk act as midwives.[30]

Post-Independence, India's affirmative policies have, however, seen members emerge as political leaders at regional and even national levels. A prominent example is Buta Singh from the Bhangi community in Punjab, who was an MP in Parliament in the early sixties and later became a Union minister of home affairs.[31] Today, the community has formed unions in the municipalities they work with, to help them be treated fairly. The objective is to strengthen the economic, social, educational and political status of all the members of the community and remove social discrimination.

Today, at a time when caste still stares us in the face, it is prudent to study Valmiki who symbolized the power of change.

What Valmiki achieved was transformation through inner will. Through introspection and honest self-reflection of where one stands, one can experience the abundant power of grace when one is open to saints and their teachings. A person can metamorphose when he is committed to personal change. Such a transformed individual alone can become a beacon of light to the world. One such individual was Ambedkar, who constantly reiterated the need to 'Educate, Organise, Agitate'.[32] Valmiki, however, teaches us the power of transformation through education and empowering oneself spiritually.

Notes

1. Martin Luther King Jr., *Strength to Love*, Fortress Press, 1981.
2. Kuldip K Dhiman, 'Introduction', *The Yogavasishta of Valmiki*, Wisdom Tree, 2019, p. 15.
3. 'Maharishi Valmiki: Composer of Shri Ramayana', Hindu Janajagruti Samiti, https://www.hindujagruti.org/articles/53.html
4. C. Bulcke, 'About Vālmīki', *Ramakatha and Other Essays*, Vani Prakashan, 2010, p. 13.
5. Rev. C. Bulcke, 'About Vālmīki', Ramakatha and Other Essays, Vani Prakashan, 2010, p. 13
6. Kuldip K. Dhiman, *The Yogavasishta of Valmiki*, Wisdom Tree, 2019, p. 16.
7. Pravin Agrawal, '16 Shocking facts about Maharishi Valmiki no one knows!', Speaking Tree, 6 October 2014, https://www.speakingtree.in/allslides/16-shocking-facts-about-maharishi-valmiki-no-one-knows/200850 (accessed on 31 March 2020).
8. Seema Burman, 'The Narada Bhakti Sutra', *Economic Times*, 14 March 2017, https://economictimes.indiatimes.com/blogs/the-speaking-tree/the-narada-bhakti-sutra/ (accessed on 31 March 2020).
9. 'Valmiki', Mahavidya, 22 April 2016, http://www.mahavidya.ca/2016/04/22/valmiki/ (accessed on 31 March 2020).
10. Bibek Debroy, 'Introduction', *The Valmiki Ramayana: Vol. 3*, Penguin Books India, 2017.

11. Kanad Sinha, 'A Tale of Three Couples and Their Poets: Ramakatha, Love and Valmiki in South Asian Tradition', *Studies in Humanities and Social Sciences*, vol. 18, nos 1–2, 2011, pp. 43–80, 2011.

12. Kuldip K. Dhiman, 'Introduction', *The Yogavasishta of Valmiki*, Wisdom Tree, 2019, p. 17; 'The Beauty of the Valmiki Ramayana by Bibek Debroy', The Penguin Digest, 29 January 2018, https://penguin.co.in/thepenguindigest/the-beauty-of-the-valmiki-ramayana-by-bibek-debroy/ (accessed on 31 March 2020).

13. Debroy, 'Introduction'.

14. Sri Aurobindo, *The Renaissance in India and Other Essays on Indian Culture*, Sri Aurobindo Ashram Publication Department, 2002.

15. Julia Leslie, *Authority and Meaning in Indian Religions: Hinduism and the Case of Valmiki*, Routledge, 2003, p. 97.

16. Ibid.

17. Ibid.

18. Ibid, p. 99.

19. Ibid.

20. C. Bulcke, 'About Vālmīki', *Ramakatha and Other Essays*, Vani Prakashan, 2010, p. 15.

21. Swami Vidyaranya, *Jivan-Mukti-Viveka of Swami Vidyaranya*, translated by Swami Moksadananda, Advaita Ashrama, 1996.

22. Dhiman, 'Introduction', *The Yogavasishta of Valmiki*, p. 17.

23. Ibid.

24. Ibid, p. 49.

25. Ibid.

26. Debroy, 'Introduction'.

27. Dhiman, 'Introduction', *The Yogavasishta of Valmiki*.

28. 'Valmiki Jayanti 2019: Photo messages and wishes for all', *Statesman*, 12 October 2019, https://www.thestatesman.com/lifestyle/valmiki-jayanti-2019-photo-messages-and-wishes-for-all-1502808534.html

29. Dilip Merala, 'Valmiki Jayanti 2017: Interesting facts about Thiruvanmiyur Valmiki Temple in Chennai', India.com, 3 October 2017, https://www.india.com/travel/articles/valmiki-jayanti-2017-interesting-facts-about-thiruvanmiyur-valmiki-temple-in-chennai-3228193/

30. 'Balmiki', People Groups of India, https://peoplegroupsindia.com/profiles/balmiki/.
31. Ibid.
32. 'Dr. Ambedkar's Final Words of Advice', Drambedkarbooks.com, 26 June 2012, https://drambedkarbooks.com/2012/06/26/dr-ambedkars-final-words-of-advice/.

Veda Vyasa

A revolutionary reformer, a path-breaking poet, a writer par excellence, a brilliant editor, an inspirational sage who institutionalized teaching with passion and an institution unto himself, Veda Vyasa is one of the central names in Indian spiritual tradition. He can be referred to as 'the first nation builder' for his creation of the *teertha-yatra* pilgrimages, for '*chitta-shuddhi*' (cleansing of the mind), that prepared the ground for national unity[1] and as someone who changed the face of a nation that is known for its spiritual philosophies and practices even in contemporary times. Veda Vyasa's extraordinary achievements are evidence that those who came from the Dalit and lower-caste communities have helped Hinduism revolutionize, reorganize and reform. Krishna Dvaipayana Veda Vyasa was a product of one of ancient India's first inter-caste unions, born to a sage, Maharishi Parashara, and a fisherwoman, Satyavati. No one would have thought that this son of unequal parents would go on to represent Hinduism and its tenets. Every year, Vyasa's birth anniversary is observed as Vyasa Purnima (full-moon day), also known as Guru Purnima in the month of Ashada (July–August) of the Hindu calendar. The day is dedicated to gurus or teachers.

The apple does not fall far from the tree, and Veda Vyasa's father, too, was a sage recognized for his immense knowledge and self-realisation. He worked tirelessly to bring order and cooperation between the different sections of society by travelling extensively and setting up ashrams to impart positive values at a time when there was a lot of discord in society and little respect between communities and castes.

Right from the time he was a child, Vyasa had a strong urge to transcend the limited and the meaningless, and venture into the unknown realms of infinitude armed with a universal outlook. He set out to present the ancient wisdom of the past in a way that it could be appreciated and absorbed by all. During his young years, there was no one equal to Vyasa.[2] He was intelligent, with a high grasping power, learning and absorbing what his father, his guru, taught him.

Vyasa was deeply committed to the service of mankind and wanted to disseminate knowledge among people. Due to his relentless contribution to Hinduism in which he outlined that knowledge was vital for self unfoldment, the positive impact of which is felt even today, Vyasa can be considered one of the most daring religious revolutionaries to have appeared in Hindu cultural history. His work has had a tremendous impact on scholars, thinkers and seekers from across the globe. In the words of German Indologist Paul Deussen:

'Love your neighbour like you love yourself': Why should I do that? The answer is not found in the Bible, but in the Vedas, namely in the great formula 'Tat Twam Asi', which in three words, communicates the underlying metaphysics: You should love your neighbour like yourself, because you yourself are your neighbour, whereas to see him as different is mere illusion.[3]

It was Vyasa, equipped with an incomparably astute intellect, who decided to give humanity the categorized and documented version of the Vedas, India's immense book of knowledge that had, until then, had only been shared orally. To compile and document that was an onerous task. His mission was not an ordinary one. He had perhaps realized that there was a definite need to pen down the treatise amid forgotten traditions and calamities, such as famines, as it would prove beneficial for the generations to come. The visionary sage not only compiled the Vedas but segregated it into the four parts that it is known to have today, namely the *Rig Veda*, the *Yajur Veda*, the *Sama Veda* and the *Atharva Veda*.

However, the systematic thinker in Vyasa was apparently not satisfied with merely classifying the entire wealth of Vedic knowledge into four volumes; in each volume he also brought about a harmonious rhythm, both in the arrangement and the classification of the contents. He divided each of the four volumes roughly into four sections: *Mantras* (chants or hymns), *Brahmanas* (rituals and rules of conduct), *Aranyakas* (methods of subjective worship) and *Upanishads* (philosophical revelations).

Arthur Schopenhauer, a German scholar who was widely read before the Second World War and discussed in public newspapers and magazines, saw in the *Upanishads* the 'fruit of the highest human knowledge and wisdom' and in their introduction into the Western world 'the greatest gift of the century'. In his writings,[4] Schopenhauer confessed that reading the *Upanishads* had been the joy of his life and later the consolation at the hour of his death. According to him, this was such a great legacy to mankind because its study purified the mind like nothing else could.[5]

Vyasa was an original thinker with astounding faculties of insight and foresight. In the words of Swami Chinmayananda, one of the first spiritual teachers to expound the knowledge of the *Upanishads* in English, 'Vyasa was one of the sages who had a vast vision of the past and the great imagination to see the future, both of which he brought forth in order to tackle the problems of decadence in his immediate present.'[6]

Was Vyasa reaching out to the people in a way they could understand? To explain how the subject should be understood, he brought to the fore the Brahmasutras, an analysis based on the essential thoughts contained in the Upanishads. While the Upanishads tell us who we are, the Brahmasutras analyse and clarify, shining a light on this most vital knowledge. The Brahmasutras are the substratum for the ancient Indian philosophy; Advaita Vedanta, which states that the divinity in one is the divinity in all. To Vyasa's credit, the Brahmasutras form the umbrella of Vedantic knowledge and studies.

Vyasa's quest to present knowledge in simplified and easily comprehensible forms was both refreshing and relentless. He seemed to be of the belief that there could always be more creative ways to reach out to people. And to accomplish that, he perhaps decided to travel extensively, engage with and speak to various sages, cutting across the length and breadth of the nation, to write the *Puranas* (mystic stories based on ancient India). Vyasa compiled and wrote all of the eighteen puranas. In Vyasa's work, one can find a unique harmony of technique, plot development, character portrayal, description of nature and cultural connections. In other words, he was the greatest producer of potboilers of the time!

David Frawley, author, teacher and founder of the American Institute of Vedic Studies, has said, 'As such, Veda Vyasa developed the foundation for Hindu dharma as it endures to the present day, with its main deity forms, philosophies and yogic paths. Yet Veda Vyasa stayed in the background and never made himself into an object of worship.'[7]

One of Vyasa's most applauded works is the Mahabharata. Along with the Ramayana, this epic poem is one of Hinduism's most eminent works. The duo lies at the core of Indian national identity and culture, spanning millennia.

The Mahabharata was written with the core objective of helping the common man understand the import of dharma, the right way of living. In the *Karna Parva* of the Mahabharata, it is aptly described in the following way, 'The very purpose of Dharma is to ensure sustainability of living beings and all those that contribute fundamentally to the cause of sustainability. Dharma is primarily intended for nourishment and development of the living beings.'[8] Vyasa first taught the great epic to his son, Sage Shuka. Later, Shuka expounded it to his disciples. Had it not been so, this mighty wealth of wisdom would have been lost to future generations.

In the 1980s, the *New York Times* published a column on how the Mahabharata continues to permeate Indian thought and spirit. The column said,

> The themes of the Mahabharata continue in politics, arts, religious cultures of today. It is said in India that there is nothing in human existence which does not have a place in the Mahabharata. It contains all the contradictions of life, and its legends and stories have been told and retold in every generation. The actual story, however, makes up only about a fourth of the work. The rest consists of digressions into ethics, philosophy, statecraft, cosmology, myth and countless other subjects.[9]

Set against the backdrop of the Mahabharata, Vyasa also produced one of India's 'FAQ' handbooks—the *Bhagavad Gita*—which teaches human beings how to practically live the subtle philosophies of everyday life. The *Bhagavad Gita* occurs in the *Bhishma Parva* of the Mahabharata, comprising eighteen chapters. It is Veda Vyasa's sheer brilliance that he translated subtle Vedic maxims in his unique way, against the intricacies of politics and the edginess of a family feud.

Vyasa's accomplishments show that birth and background do not dictate a person's accomplishments.

Vyasa's experiences teach us that when one finds oneself against a proverbial wall of disadvantage, the wealth of words can hold one in better stead than a war with weapons. The words of the wise have the power to uphold and transform humanity, and indeed create history. The onus is on us to absorb the teachings that the lives and works of such great men imparted, and to move forward with the message of harmony and integration rather than confrontation.

Notes

1. Om Prakash Sharma, 'Hindu Spiritualism: The Ancient Hindu Way, A Study in Contrast', Heritage Foundation, http://www. heritagefoundation.org.in/Download/articles/hindu_spiritualism. pdf.

2. As per the authors' interview with Swami Ramakrishnananda, Research Scholar, Amrita University and Spiritual teacher, Chinmaya Mission, Nagapattinam, Tamil Nadu.

3. Paul Deussen, in S. Radhakrishnan, *Eastern Religions and Western Thought*, second edition, Oxford University Press, 1997.

4. Annette Wilke 'Impacts and Exponents of Advaita Vedanta in the Western World - An International Perspective' by , in Sandhya Sundar and Dilip Kumar Rana, eds., *Advaitamirtam*, 2015.

5. Guru Prakash And Sudarshan Ramabadran, 'Knowledge as tool for Dalit emancipation', Millennium Post, 20 July 2016, http://www.millenniumpost.in/knowledge-as-tool-for-dalit-emancipation-154621.

6. Swami Chinmayananda, 'Vedavyas—The Versatile Genius', Chinmaya Mission, 5 October 2007, http://chinmayamission. blogspot.com/2007/10/.

7. David Frawley, 'Why Guru Purnima Is Unique to Hindu Dharma', American Institute of Vedic Studies, https://www.vedanet.com/ why-guru-purnima-is-unique-to-hindu-dharma/.

8. S.B. Pillay and Anita Pillay, *The Complete Mahabharata Vol. 7: Karna Parva, Salya Parva, Stri Parva*, first edition, Rupa Publications India, 2015.

9. Steven R. Weisman, 'Many Faces of the Mahabharata', *New York Times*, 27 October 1987, https://www.nytimes.com/1987/10/27/ arts/many-faces-of-the-mahabharata.html.

Sant Janabai

God baked pots with Gora,
Drove cattle with Chokha,
Cut grass with Savata,
Wove garments with Kabir,
Colored hide with Rohidas,
Sold meat with the butcher Sajana,
Melted gold with Narahari
Carried cow-dung with Janabai,
And even became a Pariah messenger for Damaji.'

—*Sant Eknath*[1]

When looking into the contributions and the achievements of
Dalits, a common theme that can be seen again and again is the
overcoming of oppression to excel and succeed in massive areas
of social impact, be that law, politics or education. The beauty
of Janabai's story is that she was not directly or intentionally
involved in any great initiative of change, nor was she equipped
or empowered with the worldly skills or schooling to do so. Yet,
the purity of her devotion has had such a huge impact on the
world, that the words of this Dalit poetess have indeed been

immortalised. The company of saints transformed a simple lower-caste girl into a saint herself, Sant Janabai, in a country where the epithet 'Sant' has largely been used for spiritual ideals of the male gender.

> *Jani's abhangas are composed by God himself, all the saints listen to her religiously.*
> *Blessed is Jani, blessed is her devotion.'*
>
> —*Sant Namdev*[2]

Although Janabai has been revered by so many saints and seers, her birth anniversary is never celebrated, since her date of birth has gone completely unrecorded. However, it is said that she was born around 1263 CE in rural Maharashtra, into a Shudra family, and died around 1350 CE, in her beloved town, Pandharpur.[3] Her mother died in the Gangakhed village when Janabai was very young, and her father, foreseeing a short life for himself too, took the little girl to Pandharpur, the blessed home of Lord Vitthala, an incarnation of Lord Vishnu. Lord Vitthala and his town of Pandharpur are worshipped and adored by countless devotees, especially Marathi-speaking Hindus of the Varkari (pilgrim) tradition.

At the age of seven, Janabai was left in a temple, under the protection of the deity Vitthala, where a merchant named Damasheti Shimpi mistakenly stepped on her hand. The merchant and his family were ardent devotees of Vitthala and took Janabai in to serve as a maidservant later. But rather than living a life of torture and torment, although it was difficult at times, Janabai flourished as a devotee of Lord Vitthala in the Damasheti household. One of her duties was to take care of Damasheti's son, Namdev, who went on to become one of the most famous religious poets of Maharashtra, as did Janabai herself.

Although Janabai was from a lower caste and she was appointed as Namdev's *daasi* (servant), he loved her as an elder sister, and she spent her entire life in his service. The simple and uneducated girl learnt a lot from Namdev. Through his divine poetry, he taught her that all were equal in front of the Lord, regardless of caste and gender. His words had a great influence on her, as she already had a natural love for God, her Vitthala, who had placed her in the perfect environment for her devotion to grow. Although her poetry suggests that she had a tough life of hard menial labour, she saw service as a means of spiritual upliftment. Her spirits were kept up by the constant presence of divinity in her life, thanks to her association with Namdev and the holy land of Pandharpur.

In one of her poems, Janabai beseeches God:

> Let me undergo as many births in this world as You please, but grant that my desires are fulfilled. They are that I see Pandharpur and serve Namdev in every birth. I do not mind if I am a bird or a swine, a dog or a cat, but my conditions are that in each of these lives, I must see Pandharpur and serve Namdev. This is the ambition of Namdev's maid.[4]

Namdev was the guru or the spiritual master of Janabai, and it is through him that she met several other saints. Her poems are a reflection of the intense reverence she had towards Sant Dnyaneshwar, Sant Chokhamela and, of course, Sant Namdev, all of whom were saints of the Maharashtrian Bhakti movement. By the strength of her devotion-filled words, Sant Janabai, too, has earned herself a place of reverence in the hearts of millions of seekers and devotees, and she, too, is seen as a proponent of Bhakti. History has seen women and lower castes shunned and forbidden from practising rituals for centuries on end, but the Bhakti movement was different.

Say editors Sanjay Paswan and Pramanshi Jaideva in *Encyclopedia of Dalits in India*,

The Maharastrian Bhakti movement, similar to movements throughout in India, was anti-orthodox, including both women and shudras, was based on the experience of God rather than on traditional piety or rituals. Its radical stance and its inclusiveness, however, were largely confined to the religious plane, and action for social equality from it was trivial.[5]

While the advocates of Bhakti placed more emphasis on reverence than on resistance, the subtle undercurrents of a move against the prevalent system were present throughout their poetry. These religious revolutionaries, in their own beautiful way, provided opportunities for the depressed classes to feel as comfortable paying obeisance to God as the privileged classes did. The actions of the lower castes may have been controlled by upper-caste society at the time but their devotion was encouraged in all its intensity by those at the forefront of the Bhakti movement.

The saints wrote poems and songs about God, but their works also offered a slice of real life, throwing light on the discontent and misery the lower castes felt.

Author Rajeshwari Pandharipande writes how 'the worldy life of deprivation or abundance has always been a point in a saint's life from which he/she departs or in the context of which he/she finds freedom. To put it differently, it is the worldly lives of the saints that contextualize their spiritual lives.'[6] This is why it is necessary to study Janabai in her role as a maid to Namdev, an identity that shaped her spirituality. The author also points out the three images of Janabai found in her poetry—an orphan maidservant, Namdev's maid and disciple, and a saint.[7] Janabai's poems, although so complete in their spirit of surrender, also speak of her loneliness and her longing for the Lord. The maidservant of Damasheti Shimpi's household composed these words, wrought of a sense of unfair isolation:

Your wife and mother stay at your feet and sons are placed
proudly in front, this woman is kept on the doorstep—no room
for the lowly inside.
O God, how I want your embrace! When will you call dasi Jani
your own?[8]

She felt that Lord Vitthala was always by her side and indeed
within her—the ultimate spiritual experience for any seeker. It is
said that one day, as Janabai was singing one of her compositions,
Sant Dnyaneshwar walked into the temple to see the Lord writing
something down with great focus and attention. Lord Vitthala
told Dnyaneshwar, much to the latter's amusement, that he was
writing down the words of the song, even though they were about
him! Such was the Lord's regard for his sincere devotee. Here is
the incident in Janabai's own imaginative words, as though from
the Lord's perspective:

I wrote down Jani's words as she uttered them, Jnanadeva!
Let it be known to you, this has not made me any less divine!
The absolute truth is the paper, and with ink of eternity Vitthal
writes on it, incessantly with Jani.[9]

As time passed, Janabai became more and more engrossed in
her devotion to the Lord, so much so that society, especially the
Brahmins of Pandharpur, began to mock her. It may also have
had to do with the fact that her popularity kept increasing among
the commonfolk, who could relate to her simple words, short
verses and catchy tunes, not to mention her purity and sincerity
towards God.

As Janabai grew older and became slower in performing her
household chores, the Lord himself is said to have come to her aid.
She would fall asleep at the end of a long day, only to wake up and
find out that Lord Vitthala had completed all of her work. On one

such occasion, the Lord is said to have returned to the temple in the morning covered in her blanket and missing some ornaments. When the temple priests found the ornaments at Janabai's house, all hell broke loose. They accused her of theft, and she was arrested and sentenced to death. She was ill-treated, laughed at and called a liar when she tried to explain, but nothing could shake her devotion. Her constant remembrance of the Lord and deep faith in him ensured that she was miraculously saved—it is said that the noose around her neck transformed into a garland as she chanted her Lord's name.

It is believed that Janabai breathed her last at the main entrance of the Vitthala temple at Pandharpur, a place where she was never allowed to worship on account of her low caste. It is also believed that she and Namdev left their mortal forms on the same day, so sacred and connected was their devotion to the Lord. Both discarded their physical forms to merge with God, and both live on in the hearts of numerous devotees, who continue to sing their *abhanga*s.

Janabai voiced through her poems the 'double injustice of being a woman and a sudra'.[10] She was excluded from receiving knowledge of the scriptures. Her poems have, in a way, served as a collection of her life experiences, which also happen to include details of the lives of the other saints she interacted with. This is a terrific legacy for a lower-caste woman—someone from whom society had no expectations of greatness whatsoever. It is said that Sant Namdev was so pleased with her devotion that he included her compositions in his own when it was time to compile a collection. Janabai wrote more than 300 *abhanga*s, many of which are sung even today, often during processions on foot to Pandharpur, but more often by those who perform their duties tirelessly, singing her abhangas in an attempt to remember the Lord through their activities. Just like Janabai had once said: 'I will sing your name while pounding and grinding, O Eternal One.'[11]

In 2014, more than 650 years after the passing away of Janabai, a historic verdict was passed in Pandharpur to allow priests from backward classes to perform prayers at the Vitthala temple, and to allow female priests to perform prayers at the Rukhmini temple.[12] There could be no greater tribute to the memory of the great saints of Maharashtra's Bhakti movement, who pioneered the country's efforts to bring about such a change at places of worship, by reiterating that is never any discrimination from God's side. Even though it took centuries for the decision to come about, it is a gigantic step in the right direction.

Notes

1. D.B. Mokashi, *Palkhi: An Indian Pilgrimage*, trans. by Philip C. Engblom and Eleanor Zelliot, State University of New York Press, 1987, pp. 42–43.

2. Maharashtra Navnirman Sena, 'Saint Janabai', https://web.iiit.ac.in/~sarvesh.ranadeug08/project/saints/Saintper cent20Janabai.html (accessed 19 July 2018.).

3. Manu S. Pillai, 'Opinion: The kitchen maid as Bhakti poet', *Livemint*, 19 July 2019, https://www.livemint.com/mint-lounge/features/the-kitchen-maid-as-bhakti-poet-1563506602208.html (accessed 31 March 2020).

4. Sandhya Mulchandani, *For the Love of God: Women Poet Saints of the Bhakti Movement*, Penguin Random House, 2019.

5. Sanjay Paswan and Paramanshi Jaideva, eds, *Encyclopaedia of Dalits in India: Vol. 4*, Kalpaz Publications, 2002.

6. Rajeshwari V. Pandharipande, 'Janabai: A Woman Saint of India', *Women Saints in World Religions*, ed. Arvind Sharma, State University of New York Press, 2000, p. 154.

7. Ibid, p. 155

8. Anne Feldhaus, ed., *Images of Women in Maharashtrian Literature and Religion*, State University of New York Press, 1996, pp. 218–19.

9. Arvind Sharma, ed., *Women Saints in World Religions*, State University of New York Press, 2000, (State University of New York Press, 2000), pp. 173-74.

10. Dalbir Bharti, *Women and the Law*, APH Publishing, 2008, p.6.
11. Ibid, supra cxxi.
12. 'Pandharpur temple allows female and non-female brahmin male priests,' *The Hindu*, 1 August 2014, https://www.thehindu.com/news/national/other-states/pandharpur-temple-allows-female-and-nonbrahmin-male-priests/article6272617.ece (accessed 12 January 2019).

Savitribai Phule

'An active effort to promote the rights or progress of other disadvantaged persons': This is how affirmative action has traditionally been defined and the term is recorded to have first been used in 1961.[1] If one were to carefully analyse, however, affirmative action was much earlier put to effective use in the context of Dalit-led empowerment by India's first female teacher, Savitribai Phule.

Born on 3 January 1831 in Maharashtra's Satara district, Savitribai is credited with laying the foundation for educational opportunities for women in India. She also played a major role in the struggle for women's rights in the country during the British Raj. She belonged to the *maali* (gardener) caste. The name 'Phule' owes its origins to '*phul*', meaning 'flower' in the English language.

'Savitribai was subject to intense harassment every day as she walked to the school to teach. Stones, mud and dirt were flung at her as she passed,' writes Cynthia Stephen in an essay titled 'The Stuff Legends Are Made of'.[2] Savitribai was even advised to wear an old sari while walking to school, change into a newer one before taking classes and then change back into the old sari while returning home. This was the situation in the society in Savitribai's time. Women were to be solely restricted to household work. In fact, author Dhananjay Keer records Savitribai's response to the horrific inhumane situation: 'Embarrassed by this unholy uproar and upsurge, she would stop in the street and say serenely to her persecutors: "God forgive you. I am doing my duty. May he bless you."'[3]

Savitribhai's response to cruelty was through calmness. Her focus was on fighting for the rights of the untouchables by using education as a catalyst for empowerment, and this speaks volumes about her mental equipoise and character.

This is so aptly articulated by Thom Wolf:

> Indian women owe her. For in today's world, whether an Indian school girl reading English, an Indian woman who reads, an Indian woman who is educated, or an educated international desi woman, her education as an Indian female grows from the garden planted by Savitribai Phule.[4]

All her life, Savitribai strove to liberate the shackled, the crushed and the oppressed, with a belief that every woman, every child and every man had a right to getting educated and remaking their lives.[5] In Savitribai, India witnessed a legendary female pioneer of social and gender justice in the country, and who was an epitome of Dalit-led empowerment and affirmative action on par with Ambedkar's.

In addition to championing education for the empowerment of the Dalits, Savitribai was a social worker, a writer and a poet. Most of her poems spoke about discrimination and the need to get an education. During most of her life, her relentless campaign was against sati, child marriage and social evils.

Savitribai was the eldest daughter of Lakshmi and Khandoji Neveshe Patil. At the age of nine, in 1840, she was married to thirteen-year-old Jyotirao Phule. Jyotirao educated her at home and trained her to become a teacher. Along with her husband, also a social reformer, she went on to open eighteen schools for girls, becoming India's first female teacher and headmistress. She was also instrumental in opening fifty-two boarding schools for the welfare of orphans affected during famines. The couple adopted a child, the son of a Brahmin widow, and named him Yashwant. He later went on to serve as a medical practitioner. Jyotirao and Savitribai left their joint household to begin a separate life of struggle together.

They fought the evil of casteism head-on and at various levels. So much so that every well-thought-through measure of theirs in their fight against untouchability can serve as a case study. One of Savitribai's phenomenal qualities was that she was not exclusivist. Which means that the teachers appointed in the schools run by her and Jyotirao included many from the upper castes as well, along with women and a number of men. Fatima Sheikh, who worked with Savitribai from the very beginning, is said to have been the first female Muslim teacher in a modern school in India.[6] Eventually, Savitribai and Jyotirao opened several schools for adults, agriculturalists and labourers.

Savitribai took it upon herself to lead the gender justice movement in India. She not only fought for the right to education for girls but also for the right to dignity for widows. Her contribution to education remains unparalleled. In as early as 1852, she started the Mahila Seva Mandal to fight for the rights of women. The British government honoured both Savitribai and Jyotirao in 1852 for their contribution to the cause of women's education.

Savitribai's struggle encouraged and inspired a whole generation of campaigners for gender justice in Maharashtra— Dr Anandi Bai Gopal Joshi, Pandita Ramabai, Tarabai Shinde, Ramabai Ranade and many others.[7]

Savitribai often communicated through her poems. In 1854, she published a collection that emphasized the eternal significance of education.

Be self-reliant, be industrious
Work—gather wisdom and riches,
All gets lost without knowledge
We become animal without wisdom,
Sit idle no more, go, get education
End misery of the oppressed and forsaken,
You've got a golden chance to learn
So learn and break the chains of caste.[8]

In his speeches, Jyotirao credited Savitribai and her contribution to starting India's first all-girl school. In those days, for a man to credit a woman, especially in educational matters, was unheard of. But here was a couple that broke traditional and orthodox barriers in great fashion. In the words of Jyotirao Phule:

> My experience in educational matters is principally confined to Poona (Pune) and the surrounding villages. About 25 years ago, the missionaries had established a female school at Poona but no indigenous school for girls existed at the time. I, therefore, was induced about the year 1854 to establish such a school, and in which I and my wife worked together for many years.[9]

Savitribai started a school with Sagunabai, who was a child widow and a mentor, in Maharwada in 1847. Fondly called 'Aai Maa' (aunt mother), Sagunabai left deep imprints in the minds of the Phules, who gratefully acknowledged her as the greatest and most ennobling influence in their lives.

Later, on 1 January 1948, the country's first school for girls was started at Bhide Wada in Pune and Savitribai was nominated as the first headmistress of the school. At a time when teaching girls was not common, especially for the oppressed classes, Savitribai fearlessly went ahead to did just that. She undertook training at Ms. Farar's Institution in Ahmednagar and in Ms. Mitchell's school in Pune.[10]

Savitribai's contribution to Dalit literature remains largely understudied. She penned a collection of poems titled *Kavya Phule*[11] and *Bavan Kashi Subodh Ratnakar* (*The Ocean of Pure Gems*) in 1891[12], as well as essays such as *Karz*, which focuses on the issue of debt. Her literary work documents the sociopolitical climate of the time, touching on issues such as education, caste and the liberation of untouchables. Savitribai's remarkable influence and success in running her schools is evident. A young girl, Mukta Salve, wrote an essay, 'Mang Maharachya Dukhvisayi',[13] which translates to 'Grief of the Mangs and Mahars', which was published in the paper *Dyanodaya* in 1855—the quality of this essay showcased the level of education imparted in Savitribai's schools. Savitribai motivated the eleven-year-old Muktabai to write this essay, which became the cornerstone of Dalit literature. It portrays the atrocities committed against untouchables and received accolades even for its English translation—it is considered one of the earlier works in Dalit literature.[14]

Citing education as the main catalyst for change and empowerment, Muktabai writes in the article:

> Oh, the mahars and mangs, you are poor and sick. Only the medicine of knowledge will cure and heal you. You will become righteous and moral. It will stop your exploitation. People who treat you like animals will not dare to treat like that anymore. So please work hard and study.[15]

The writer's lambasting of the caste system, and the religion that upholds it, reveals the 'potential explosiveness' of education that both Savitribai and Jyotirao were so keen to create.

Savitribai was an audacious revolutionary. She was also the first woman in the history of India to enter the male bastion and light her husband's funeral pyre.[16] Her choice to do so sent shock waves across the land then. Another remarkable moment in her life was when she organized a strike against barbers in Pune and

Bombay, putting pressure on them to stop shaving the heads of Brahmin widows. She supported widow remarriage and was against child marriage. In one of her letters to Jyotirao,[17] she mentioned coming to the aid of a couple going for an inter-caste marriage by convincing people to not kill the Brahmin boy. Inter-caste marriages were later cited by Ambedkar as an important tool to annihilate the caste system.[18] To support such marriages in the late nineteenth century required exemplary courage and commitment.

After Jyotibai's death, Savitribai took on the mantle of leading the Satyashodhak Samaj. She was already looking after its day-to-day functioning as the head of its women's wing. She presided over the 1893 session of the *samaj* and led from the front during the famine and plague epidemic in 1896–97.[19]

Savitribai died on 10 March 1897, having contracted the plague from patients at the clinic run by her and her son. To honour female social reformers, the government of Maharashtra has instituted an award in her name. A stamp was released by India Post in her honour on 10 March 1998. Recently, the Maharashtra government paid a rich tribute to India's first female teacher by naming Pune University after her. During her long and illustrious public life, Savitribai is credited with having been one of the first women to be published in India—she published four books, including two volumes of poetry. She also headed the Satyashodhak Samaj after Jyotirao Phule and broke new ground in social cohesion.[20]

Braj Ranjan Mani, a noted scholar of subaltern studies, writes:

Savitribai Phule struggled and suffered with her revolutionary husband in an equal measure, but remains obscured due to casteist and sexist negligence. Apart from her identity as Jyotirao Phule's wife, she is little known even in academia. Modern India's first woman teacher, a radical exponent of mass and female education, a champion of women's liberation, a pioneer of engaged poetry, a courageous mass leader who took on the forces of caste and patriarchy certainly had her independent identity and contribution. It is indeed a measure of the ruthlessness of elite-controlled knowledge production that a figure as important as Savitribai Phule fails to find any mention in the history of modern India.[21]

Caste and gender-based exclusion forms the nucleus of marginalized narrative in postcolonial academic imagination. That is why the role of Savitribai Phule was so vital, and that is why she was aptly called 'Krantijyoti', or the lamp of revolution. Now is the time to contemplate her contributions and the contributions of others like her who followed later—those who dedicated their lives to the cause of Dalit women, especially through education.

Notes

1. Linda Holtzman and Leon Sharpe, *Media Messages: What Film, Television, and Popular Music Teach Us About Race, Class, Gender, and Sexual Orientation*, M.E. Sharpe, 2014, p. 396.

2. Cynthia Stephen, 'The Stuff Legends Are Made of', in Braj Ranjan Mani and Pamela Sardar, *A Forgotten Liberator*, Mountainpeak, 2013.

3. Dhananjay Keer, *Mahatma Jotirao Phooley: Father of the Indian Social Revolution*, Popular Prakashan, 1997, p. 26.

4. Thom Wolf, 'Comenius and Savitribai Phule', *Journal of Applied Christian Leadership*, vol. 5, no. 2, 2011.

5. Braj Ranjan Mani and Pamela Sardar, eds, *A Forgotten Liberator: The Life and Struggle of Savitribai Phule*, Mountain Peak, 2013, 2015.

6. Divya Kandukuri, 'The life and times of Savitribai Phule', *Livemint*, 11 January 2019, https://www.livemint.com/Leisure/DmR1fQSnVD62p4D3eyq9mO/The-life-and-times-of-Savitribai-Phule.html.

7. Mani and Sardar, eds, *A Forgotten Liberator*, p. 10.

8. Ibid.

9. Karthik Venkatesh, 'Education for Liberation: Exploring Mahtama Phule's Work in Education', *Sage Journals*, 14 December 2015.

10. 'Savitribai Phule as a tradition breaker: The first female teacher at the first girls' school', *India Today*, 3 January 2017, https://www.indiatoday.in/education-today/gk-current-affairs/story/savitribai-phule-952878-2017-01-03.

11. Supra cxxx.

12. Savitribai Phule, *Bavan Kashi Subodh Ratnakar*, 1982.

13. Savitribai Phule, 'Mang Maharachya Dukhvisayi', in Braj Ranjan Mani and Pamela Sardar (eds.), *A Forgotten Liberator*.

14. Aishwarya Javalgekar, 'Mukta Salve: The Firest Female Dalit Writer', Feminism in India, 20 March 2017, https://feminisminindia.com/2017/03/20/mukta-salve-essay/.

15. Savitribai Phule, 'Mang Maharachya Dukhvisayi', in Braj Ranjan Mani and Pamela Sardar, eds, *A Forgotten Liberator*.

16. Divya Kandukuri, 'The life and times of Savitribai Phule'. *Livemint*. 11 January 2019. https://www.livemint.com/Leisure/DmR1fQSnVD62p4D3eyq9mO/The-life-and-times-of-Savitribai-Phule.html (accessed on 12 Jan 2019).

17. Savitribai Phule, 'Mang Maharachya Dukhvisayi', in Braj Ranjan Mani Pamela Sardar, *A Forgotten Liberator*.

18. B.R. Ambedkar, *Annihilation of Caste* (first published May 1936, Blumoon Books, 2000).

19. Mani and Sardar, eds, *A Forgotten Liberator*, pp. 10-11.

20. Ibid., p. 14.

21. Id.

Soyarabai

For ages, women from socially segregated minorities have been denied basic human dignities. Thousands of Dalit women even today are abducted, raped, murdered or burnt every year. Thousands are mistreated, spoken down to, spoken ill of, considered to be other people's property or subjected to other misdeeds of prejudice. One cannot even imagine it, but this is a much improved scenario, compared with what was handed down through the centuries. Today, while things are still terrible for Dalit women, there are NGOs, a few columnists, ambassadors and others who are willing to speak up for their rights. Today, although there is a long way to go, women are being encouraged and empowered to raise their voices against oppression. This was definitely not the case in the thirteenth and the fourteenth centuries.

From the dusty settlement of Mangalvedha in Maharashtra emerged one of India's most eminent role models, the ever-positive and pragmatic wife of Chokha Mela, Soyarabai. Chokha Mela was a contemporary of Sant Dyaneshwar and Sant Namdev (AD 1275–AD 1297).[1]

Soyarabai's exact date of birth is not known. In fact, very little is known about this wonderful human being. However, the one thing that emerges about the way she led her life, from the few details available, is that she eptiomized devotion. Her story speaks of how even ruins can lead to transformation. Not only was she an enabler in Chokha Mela's life, she also engrained noble virtues in their son Karma Mela. Soyarabai premised her own life on integrity and honesty. A pertinent incident related to this can be recalled here.

Soyarabai, a child bride from a Mahar family, joined her husband and mother-in-law in their small home in Maharwada after she reached puberty. One afternoon, her mother-in-law sent her to collect firewood from the nearby forest. Being protective of the new bride and not wanting her to go alone, she asked her to join two local women, Drupadi and Ithi, who were also going to collect firewood from there. As they walked, the two women indulged in mindless chatter about their everyday lives—their chores, their marital woes, complaints about their mothers-in-law. Young Soyarabai had nothing to contribute to the conversation, so she just listened.[2]

Before long, the three were stopped by two men who made unwelcome advances at them. Soyarabai bristled when she heard their suggestive words. After some time, Ithi accompanied one of the men home. Soyarabai could not understand what was happening, so Drupadi explained it to her. While upper-caste men shunned even the shadow of a lower-caste person and refused to drink water offered by them, they had no problem using a lower-caste woman to satisfy their carnal desires. A higher caste did not amount to higher or nobler values, as adultery was rampant in the so-called higher-caste households. Women like Ithi and Drupadi had come to understand and accept this as a way of life. Soyarabai was shocked—she would have none of it. Although it was impossible to stand up to anyone from an upper caste in those days, she vowed to protect her honour.[3]

Her parents and in-laws, especially her husband, were great devotees of Panduranga Vitthala, a much-worshipped form of

Vishnu, whose abode was the nearby holy town of Pandharpur. Chokha, although from a very poor family, was of noble thought and deed, was a regular visitor to Pandharpur with his father. When they were married, Soyarabai's father, Krishna, wanted no dowry—he, in fact, offered to get his son, Banka, married to Chokha's sister, Nirmala. Both the couples would go on to be celebrated and revered as heroes of the Bhakti Movement, thanks to their timeless *abhanga*s, or devotional Marathi poems.[4]

The double marriage took place, and Soyarabai and Nirmala stayed at their own homes until they came of age.

A turning point in Soyarabai's life came when Nivritti Yeskar, Chokha's father, passed away. One day, news came to Mehunpur that he had breathed his last while taking the name of Vitthala. Krishna, Chokha's father-in-law, rushed to Mangalvedha with Soyarabai so she could help her mother-in-law cope with the loss.[5] While a similar situation would have spelt doom for many other girls of similar age, Soyarabai's in-laws quashed every stereotype by their devotion to Vitthala. Meera adored her daughter-in-law and would praise her more than even Nirmala. The teenage groom, Chokha, was loving and attentive. He shared his beautiful words of devotion with her and though their lives could in no way be called easy, the tremendous sense of blessedness kept them at peace. Together they offered their devotion to Vitthala, and that formed a special bond between them.

Theirs was a simple, religious life, with fasts observed every Ekadashi (the eleventh day of every fortnight), a lamp lit at the tulsi vrindavana in the courtyard every evening, abhangas and bhajans being sung, and a clean house. In their home there were no quarrels, no foul language used, no case of domestic violence, no liquor or meat consumed, no craving for any extravagance, no gossip and no untoward behaviour of any kind. They showed their love for each other in simple ways. Soyarabai's love for Chokha knew no bounds; she was always in awe of his purity. It is believed that she would mentally offer her husband *arati* every day.When Chokha came back from a hard day of work lifting animal carcasses, sweeping roads, disposing of garbage and breaking firewood, Soyarabai would have warm water ready for him to freshen up. She would also serve him a jaggery drink and massage his exhausted legs and feet.

They had little but they made do, and even shared what they had with those who were needier than them. One day, Soyarabai and Nirmala were sweeping the courtyard when a stranger, Ramu Ramoshi, approached them to ask for shelter, as he said he was running from the police.[6] Something about him seemed genuine and Soyarabai allowed him to hide in the haystack in the backyard but warned him that she would cut him into pieces with her Mahar's sickle if it turned out that he had committed a crime. The police came looking for him and informed the women that he was a murderer. They did not blow his cover but when the police had gone, they firmly asked him to leave. Ramu explained that he had indeed killed a moneylender, but only because he had accosted his wife in a field and he had to defend her honour. They offered him water and a meal before he continued on his way. Soyarabai's courage and compassion were appreciated by both her mother-in-law and her sister-in-law.[7]

As time passed, Soyarabai became more and more devout and would often accompany Chokha to Pandharpur. There she met Janabai, who was like a sister to her and also a mentor. Every moment spent in Pandharpur was like a balm on the wounds of ill treatment they received in Mangalvedha. Soyarabai accepted this ill treatment meted out to her and her family with tolerance, and without anger or bitterness. In time it would be she who made Chokha Mela understand and shape his responses to a situation by drawing on the wisdom he had inculcated in her. Her calm disposition and her ability to experience the divine in everyday life meant that she rarely lamented her lot on life. This is one of the key lessons we can learn from her in contemporary times.

Such purity finds itself rewarded in one way or another. After a visit to Pandharpur, she experienced a great surge in devotion and began writing poems. One day, there was a knock on the door when she was alone. An upper-caste Vaishnav was standing there. He had heard her singing a devotional song and thought he would ask for something to eat and drink, as he had not had anything all day. But Soyarabai was flummoxed as it was unheard of for a Mahar to offer anything to a Vaishnav. But when he beseeched her, she rushed to get him the only food they had at home—rice and curd. The man was touched by her kindness and blessed her as he left, placing on her open palm some of the curd rice from his own meal.[8] The next Ekadashi, she discovered that she was expecting a child, after wishing and waiting for so long. She believed it was Vitthala's grace being showered upon her and Chokha, that he had come to their house disguised as the Vaishnav and had given her his blessings in the form of the curd rice he had left in her open palm.

Soyarabai felt blessed to be associated with people such as Sant Namdev, whom Chokha took to be his guru. In fact, the more time she spent with Namdev and Janabai, the more she felt empowered, inspired and closer to Vitthala in her heart. Her conversations with Chokha and her own introspection helped her experience God's grace more with every passing day.

Every time Soyara would wonder how she would deliver her child, since both her mother and her mother-in-law were dead by then, she would think of Vitthala and ask Him to take care of her. Her earnest prayers seem to have reached Him—when Soyara was alone at the time she went into labour, He came to her in the form of Nirmala. However, it is said that Chokha was with Banka and Nirmala at the time, revelling in the bliss of satsang for a full month. For the whole of the month it is believed that Vitthala stayed with Soyarabai. Not only did he deliver her baby but he also bathed both of them, fed her, cleaned the house, cooked, looked after the newborn and attended to visitors. He even gave the baby the name Karma. Soyarabai was amazed at how attentive Nirmala was, not realizing it was her Vitthala all the while. When Chokha returned from one of his Pandharpur journeys, and they exchanged stories, they were overwhelmed by love and gratitude for Vitthala.[9]

One day, as Chokha and Soyarabai were returning from Pandharpur, they saw an elderly couple from the Mang community, considered even lower than the Mahars, walking wearily and unsteadily with loads on their heads. Soyarabai rushed to help them, not thinking of what others around them would say. After all, interacting with a lower caste was considered taboo. But true to her character, not only did she give them water but also comforted them with her kind words.[10]

So blessed was their family that not only Chokha, Soyarabai, Banka and Nirmala, but even Karma grew up with devotional words on his lips. Young Karma would undertake the difficult journey to Pandharpur on foot with his parents, singing all the way with the other *varkari*s (pilgrims), and with black ash smeared on his forehead. Black is considered an inclusive colour, as all other shades can be absorbed in it. Applying black ash on one's forehead is a sign that devotion has no room for discrimination—the focus is on God alone.

Unlike his parents, Karma was less forgiving of the unfair treatment meted out to the lower castes. He questioned every act of discrimination and expressed his anger and distaste openly. His parents showered only love on him and taught him gentleness and compassion, leading by example. They tempered his frustration with their love for Vitthala. Soyarabai told Karma that negative feelings would only harden his heart and that anger and pain would eat away at him from inside. Instead, she advised him to use his energies to remember God in all the love and devotion he could muster. Her words and her deep faith did the trick, and Karma dropped his anger to embrace the Bhakti Movement.[11]

Not much has been written about Soyarabai's life after the death of Chokha in 1338, but, needless to say, she would have remained immersed in divine thoughts until she, too, would have left her mortal form to merge into infinitude with her Vitthala.

Soyarabai's contribution to the overarching Dalit movement cannot be missed. She, along with Chokha Mela, were among the key catalysts of the Varkari movement, which was premised on the practice of social equity. In fact, this movement also gave rise to the custom of greeting people by touching their feet. The practice of ethical values, the perception of universal equality, Bhakti (devotion) and love became the four tenets of the Varkari movement. Soyarabai believed that such tenets would enable souls to evolve.[12]

Soyarabai attained sainthood by practising the noblest and simplest of virtues and values that are recognized by everyone but lived by only a few. She lived in an exploitative time, but her life was a lesson to all. Without strongly enforcing any right for herself or her family, she attained the company of not just saints but of divinity itself, by staying uncompromisingly true to her beliefs and value system. Her life can give hope and faith to the distressed and the oppressed.

Soyarabai never challenged caste and never bore any ill will towards Brahmins or any upper caste. While her life is evidence that she did not appreciate the fact that only Brahmins or those from the upper castes were considered fit enough to have access to God, her own love for Vitthala was unparalleled. She posited devotion as an equal alternative to ritual and philosophy. To date, the Varkari movement has been a formidable social enabler for the Dalits in Maharashtra, enabling holistic social cohesion.[13]

Soyarabai's story is meant for the Indian who wants to go beyond challenges to make something of his or her life. Hers was an extraordinary life spent waging a lifelong peaceful war against caste discrimination at the grass roots—overcoming social division with utter devotion.

Notes

1. Leela Gole, *Sant Chokha Mela*, translated by Shyamsunder Chandavarkar, Anmol Prakashan, 2015.
2. Gole, *Sant Chokha Mela*, p. 59.
3. Ibid., p. 59.
4. Id., pp. 19, 20.
5. Id., p. 47.
6. Id., p. 87.
7. Id., pp. 89, 90.
8. Id., p. 107.
9. Id., pp. 157–61.
10. Id., p. 209.
11. Id., p. 244.
12. Id., p. 186.
13. Sujata Anandan, 'Gujarat Dalits to dump "armed" gods, says activist Prakash Ambedkar', *Hindustan Times*, 6 August 2016, https://www.hindustantimes.com/india-news/gujarat-dalits-to-dump-armed-gods-says-activist-prakash-ambedkar/story-9KiR0EeSHmwPhB6QOvp2DK.html

Udham Singh

Udham Singh, Sher Singh, Ude Singh, Udhan Singh, Bawa, Udaan Singh, U.S. Sidhu, Mohan Singh, U.S. Azad, Frank Brazil, Singh Azad and Mohammad Singh Azad are just some of the names this patriot revolutionary was known by in his lifetime.[1]

Ambitious, passionate, fearless, relentless, focused, self-made, jovial and unpredictable are some of the characteristics that come to mind when we think of Udham Singh—for '*udham*' in itself means 'upheaval' in Punjabi.[2]

Born on 26 December 1899 in Sunam in Punjab, to parents Narain Kaur and Tehal Singh,[3] he was one of the foremost revolutionaries during the Indian freedom movement to have dealt a body blow to the British Raj. He executed a mastermind plan to avenge the merciless killings in the Jallianwala Bagh massacre. The Raj was left stunned at how he killed Sir Michael O'Dwyer and hurt the then secretary of state, Lord Zetland.

What has always enthused us as researchers is what stirred Udham to take up a risky and unpredictable journey beyond the shores of India to unexplored theatres to kill O'Dwyer, the former lieutenant governor of Punjab during the British Raj. Who supported him? What was he like as a person? Why did he do what he did?

While there are multiple accounts of whether Udham was present at the time of the Jallianwala Bagh massacre,[4] we believe that the dastardly massacre was the sole motivation behind Udham's resolve to kill those responsible for it.[5] In fact, Udham, in one of his prison discussions with educationist and Christian priest W.E.S. Holland, also mentioned the Jallianwala Bagh and his vow to take revenge on O'Dwyer, whom he considered the real culprit.[6]

Indian historians believe that Udham was indeed present when the massacre happened and helped evacuate the bodies and offered water to the injured after the shooting.[7]

The shooting, according to Indian accounts, is said to have killed more than 1000 and injured more than 1,500; and according to British accounts, it is said to have killed 379 and injured more than 1000. It is also estimated that 15,000– 20,000 people were inside the Jallianwala Bagh when the massacre took place.[8]

Udham held the then governor of Punjab, O'Dwyer (the one who gave the approval for the shooting), and then brigadier general Reginald Dyer (the one who ordered his men to shoot) responsible for the massacre, as it was under their watch that the heartless killings took place.[9] He considered his fellow citizens family and watching so many of them, including pregnant women and children, die in such a merciless way left him infuriated. He vowed to avenge the massacre and spark a revolution against the British Raj so that such a killing would never take place again. We believe this was not about himself but about his nation and its people. He was willing to lay down his life for the cause, as is evident from his final words, 'I am not afraid to die. I am proud to die. I hope that in my place will come thousands of my countrymen to drive you dirty dogs out; to free my country.'[10] These were the words he spoke when he was awarded the death sentence for the killing of O'Dwyer.

It is imperative to note here that Dyer, who was forced to resign from the army subsequent to the Hunter Commission report, thanks to the Indian representation in it,[11] suffered a stroke in 1921 and succumbed to another on 23 July 1927.[12] The Hunter Commission did not, unfortunately, implicate O'Dwyer in the Jallainwala Bagh massacre.[13] As a result, Udham set his sights on him.

The lower-caste 'Kamboj' family that Udham was born into had to face the worst kind of social discrimination, as they were not allowed to drink water from the same wells as the upper caste nor worship in the same temples. Neither did upper-caste children play with those from the lower caste.[14] Udham, named Sher Singh when he was born, fought poverty as he grew up. When he lost his mother at three,[15] his father had no choice but to work for the British as a labourer carving out Punjab's canal system. However, he too died when Udham was seven years old.[16]

Soon after, Udham was admitted into the Central Khalsa Orphanage in Amritsar with his elder brother, Sadhu Singh. It is here that he was given the name 'Udham'.[17] His brother died a few years later, in 1917, leaving Udham with no immediate living relatives.[18] Being raised in an orphanage ingrained in him a grit and independence that went on to stand him in good stead later during the Independence struggle.

Udham took to carpentry at the orphanage, but after his brother's death, he developed a strong urge to join the army under the British Raj as he needed money, food, clothing and shelter. He joined the 32nd Sikh Pioneers, which was largely made up of Dalit Sikhs.[19] His first posting was in Basra, where he was ordered to keep the railways running and then lieutenant general Sir Stanley Maude's boats afloat. This did not quite turn out the way Udham had expected and he was soon sent back, as the army found him unfit for the job.[20] But this did not deter Udham—he continued to apply to the army, for he believed that was his true calling. He was then posted as a carpenter in the army in Baghdad for the Three Works Company, where he worked for a full year.[21]

After the Jallainwala Bagh Massacre, even though his mind was filled with rage, Udham was still fighting to make ends meet. But it is at this stage in his life that he decided to travel to Africa, specifically to east Africa, where he decided to take up a job at the Ugandan Railway Company.[22]

After a while, an opportunity to join the Ghadar Party and its network came Udham's way. The Ghadar party organized Indians living overseas to identify with the Indian cause and work towards overthrowing British rule in their motherland. To this, they also distributed pamphlets and literature in India—and Udham started his career in the Ghadar Party as a leaflet boy.[23]

The Ghadar Party played a significant role in the Indian freedom movement. It is to this effect that the party started recruiting revolutionaries who would work towards its set objective. There were some inspiring methods through which they recruited people. On such was the 'Wanted Column' in the Ghadar Party literature, encouraging people to join them. The announcement contained the following:

> Wanted—enthusiastic and heroic soldiers for organising Ghadar in Hindustan.
> Remuneration—Death
> Rewards—Martyrdom
> Pension—Freedom
> Field of Work—Hindustan[24]

The role played by the Sikhs in the Ghadar Party, in their pursuit of an independent, strong and united India, was prominent. And more than 50 per cent of them were Dalits.[25]

Udham was certain that the onus was on him to get justice for the innocents killed during the Jallianwala Bagh massacre. He moved to the UK, then Mexico and finally smuggled himself into the US with the help of the Ghadar Party.[26] It was in the US that Udham got married to 'Lupe' Singh, the daughter of a landowner. However, he eventually abandoned her on one of their ship journeys and never returned to her. The Ghadar network also helped him get jobs while in the US, where he worked in the Douglas Aircraft Company.[27] It is believed that he changed his name to Frank Brazil, because the company would only allow naturalized Americans to work with it. Udham subsequently worked for the car company Ford as well.[28]

He continued to stay connected to the Ghadar Party and acted according to their plans. His journeys in eastern Europe and Morocco, of which there is little record, evidence this.[29] His Ghadar career enabled him to travel to several countries, such as Russia, France and Belgium.[30] What exactly he did in these countries as part of the Ghadar Party remains largely unknown, but here was an internationalist who did know how to speak fluent English but learnt it all by himself through these journeys. In fact, it is said there was no country in the world, except Australia, that he did not visit.[31]

It was during Udham's jail term in India for approximately five years, for having been caught with Ghadar Party propaganda,[32] that he came in contact with and was greatly influenced by one of the most dynamic revolutionaries of the time, Bhagat Singh.[33] In fact, he revered him as his guru.[34] Mohan Dass Namishray, in his book *Dalit Freedom Fighters*, writes that Udham considered Bhagat Singh his inspiration, teacher and best friend, despite being older to him. Some records say that the only photo he carried in his wallet was of Bhagat Singh and considered him the only religion he would follow.[35] But other accounts say that Udham followed the tenets of Sikhism until his very last moments.[36]

Udham wore various hats, had various aliases and used multiple addresses, but never stayed at any particular address for too long. While in England, he tried his hand at acting, when he made an appearance in the film *Elephant Boy* in 1936.[37]

When he was finally back in England to fulfil his mission of avenging the Jallianwala Bagh massacre, he used the name

Mohammad Singh Azad. Udham's much-awaited moment came on 13 March 1940. On that day, at 3 p.m. at Caxton Hall, London, a meeting of the East India Association was being held in conjunction with the Royal Central Asian Society, titled 'Afghanistan, the Present Position'.[38] O'Dwyer was not speaking at the event but chose to be present for the lecture. As per some records, Udham sat a few rows behind him.[39]

On the number of people present that day for the lecture at Caxton Hall, one account has estimated it to be 130,[40] and another 400.[41]

As the meeting came to a close, Udham got up and walked towards the speakers' platform, firing two deadly shots from his gun. The bullets killed O'Dwyer immediately. Amongst those injured were Lord Zetland, the Secretary of State for India then, who was presiding over the meeting, and Lord Lamington, former governor of Bombay, and Sir Louis Dane, O'Dwyer's predecessor in Punjab.[42]

Udham made no attempt to escape and was overpowered with the smoking revolver still in his hands. The German newspaper, *Berliner Zeitung*, called the act 'the touch of the Indian fight for freedom'.[43] They even went on to term O'Dwyer as one of Punjab's most bloodthirsty governors. The press in England linked the assassination to the Jallianwala Bagh massacre, while Indian leaders such as Mahatma Gandhi and Jawaharlal Nehru differed, maintaining that the assassination was regretted.[44]

On 1 April 1940, Udham was formally charged with the murder of O'Dwyer. Imprisoned at Brixton in London, he went on a hunger strike inside jail. He was force-fed to be kept alive. His court trial began on 4 June 1940 at the Central Criminal Court at Old Bailey. When asked why he did it, he said,

Machine guns on the streets of India mow down thousands of poor woman and children wherever your so called flag of Democracy and Christianity flies. I am against the British Imperialist Government. I am protesting. This is what I mean.

I do not care about the sentence of death. It means nothing at
all. I do not care about dying or anything.[45]

Such was his love for India and Indians. His last words before he
left the dock at the court were, 'Inquilab Zindabad! Down with
British Imperialism. Down with British dirty dogs.'[46]

There can be a perception that Udham was against the people
of Britain in general. However, his anger was guided only towards
the British government in India. 'I have nothing against the
British people at all. I have more English friends living in England
than I have in India. My greatest sympathies with the workers of
England. I am against the Imperialist Government,' he said.[47]

In prison, Udham tried to escape but his attempt was foiled by
a British mole among those he knew in prison.[48] Despite all kinds
of hardship in jail, Udham kept in touch with his confidantes and
comrades through letters.[49]

Udham was convicted by the British and sentenced to death.
On 31 July 1940, he was hanged at Pentonville Prison. Like
his guru Bhagat Singh, Udham kissed the noose before he was
hanged.[50]

On 19 July 1974, thirty-five years since his martyrdom, his
remains were exhumed and returned to India. The casket was
received with due respect by Shankar Dayal Sharma (president of
the INC then) and Zail Singh (chief minister of Punjab).[51] Prime
Minister Indira Gandhi laid a wreath on it.[52] Udham's body was
then carried in a procession through all the major towns of Punjab
and cremated in his birthtown, Sunam.[53] Much of his ashes
were immersed in the Ganges, while the rest were preserved at
Jallianwala Bagh in Amritsar, as it is here that his mission began.[54]
In 2018, a statue of Udham Singh was unveiled outside Jallianwala
Bagh.[55]

Udham was a tough man who fought poverty throughout
his life while practically having no support system. In essence,
he wrote his own chapters the way he wanted. His actions show

that there was always a discreetness in the way he operated, which amounted to his avenging of the Jallianwala Bagh massacre.

Staying steadfast in one's goals is one of the key lessons that we can imbibe from the life of Udham Singh. Yes, he chose a violent retribution, but the context and the reason was the massacre of innocents—he saw murder right before his eyes and decided to punish the one responsible for it. He was not formally educated but to exhibit this kind of grit and passion at such a young age speaks volumes about the man he was. His life lesson is both inspirational and aspirational.

His swiftness, sharpness and fearlessness ensured that he could get out of his comfort zone for a cause he believed in. He travelled from small, dusty towns to bustling global cities to see his mission to fruition. Bhagat Singh definitely tops the list of revolutionary names from Punjab, but Udham's contribution can never be overlooked.

Today, Punjab is the state with the highest proportion of SCs in India. Thus, it becomes all the more important to perpetuate the legacy of Udham Singh, who belonged to a disadvantaged section of society. Here is a hero who rose from nothing to avenge the deaths of thousands in the Jallianwala Bagh massacre, a tragedy that shook the national conscience. As members of civil society, it is our duty to pay respect to a great soul who became a national braveheart, but who is, sadly, yet to find a place in history.

Notes

1. These are some of the names of Udham Singh we came across in two books: Rakesh Kumar, *Udham Singh: Hero in the Cause of Indian Freedom*, Chintan Prakashan, 2019; Anita Anand, *The Patient Assassin*, Simon & Schuster, 2019.
2. Anand, *The Patient Assassin*, p. 36.
3. Ibid., p. 31.
4. Id., p. 110.
5. Id., p. 112.

6. Id., p. 12.
7. Sikander Singh, *A Great Patriot and Martyr Udham Singh*, Unistar Books : 2013, Forward by Kushwant Singh, Pg. 12-13
8. Anand, *The Patient Assassin*, p. 104.
9. Ibid., p. 3.
10. Singh, *The Trial of Udham Singh*, p. 115
11. Anand, *The Patient Assassin*, p. 140.
12. Ibid., p. 185.
13. Id., p. 140.
14. Id., p. 31.
15. Id., p. 32.
16. Id., p. 35.
17. Id., pp. 32, 33.
18. Id., p. 35.
19. Id., pp. 57, 58.
20. Id., pp. 59, 60.
21. Id., p. 61.
22. Id., p. 130.
23. Id., p. 69.
24. Mohan Dass Namishray, *Dalit Freedom Fighters*, Gyan Publishing House, New Delhi, 2010, p. 55
25. Anand, *The Patient Assassin*, p. 47.
26. Ibid., pp. 158–66.
27. Id., p. 169.
28. Id., p. 173.
29. Id., p. 181.
30. Id., pp. 208–09.
31. Singh, *A Great Patriot and Martyr Udham Singh*, p. 266.
32. Anand, *The Patient Assassin*, p. 183.
33. Ibid., p. 200.
34. Id., p. 200.
35. Id., p. 201.
36. Singh, *A Great Patriot and Martyr Udham Singh*, p. 253.
37. Anand, *The Patient Assassin*, p. 224.
38. Ibid., p. 259.
39. Id., pp. 260–61.
40. Id., p. 259.

41. Singh, *A Great Patriot and Martyr Udham Singh*, p. 136.
42. Anand, *The Patient Assassin*, pp. 260–66.
43. Mohan Dass Namishray, Dalit Freedom Fighters (Gyan Publishing House New Delhi, 2010), p. 66
44. Ibid., pp. 67,68
45. Singh, *A Great Patriot and Martyr Udham Singh*, pp. 14–15.
46. Ibid., p. 16.
47. Id., p. 15.
48. Id., p. 203.
49. Id., p. 267.
50. Id., p. 240.
51. Id., p. 310.
52. Anand, *The Patient Assassin*, p. 311.
53. Ibid., p. 311.
54. Id., pp. 312–133.
55. Id., p. 313.

B.R. Ambedkar

Bhagwan Das, author of *In Pursuit of Ambedkar*, says:

> The newspaper used to publish a lot of things about Gandhi, Jawaharlal Nehru, Azad, Subhas Chandra Bose and Jinnah but hardly a thing about the untouchable communities. I used to wonder, 'Who is our leader?' I asked Abba this, and he replied, 'Umeedkar, the one who brings hope,' which is how Abba saw Babasaheb Ambedkar.[1]

Original thinker, scholar, jurist, legislator, economist, public policy leader, development practitioner and chief architect of the Indian Constitution, Bhimrao Ramji Ambedkar was all this and more.

His thoughts were crisp, his views precise and clear, and words unabashed and unapologetic on every platform he spoke from. The more one reads about Ambedkar, the more one admires his unique intellect and understands his significance, the circumstances under which he jolted the status quo and truly sought disruption in calling for complete annihilation of the caste system.

Ambedkar saw society like no one else from the prism of brute force and caste-based discrimination. Thus, he stood for the cause of all-round empowerment of the socially disadvantaged till his very last breath. Even when he was on his way to England for the first roundtable conference in 1930, it is recorded that he wrote in a letter to 'Dadasaheb' Bhaurao Gaikwad how the people there were sympathetic towards him and that he was happy to see them inclined to favour the demands of the untouchables.[2]

As a child, Ambedkar, a Mahar, was made to sit separately in primary school because of his caste.[3] When someone served him water, it was from a height to avoid physical contact with him; he was even denied a haircut because he hailed from the Mahar community.[4] All this is just a glimpse of the treacherous discrimination that a six-year-old Dalit child had to go through.

Who would have thought then that this child, born on 14 April 1891 in the tiny military village of Mhow, would one day establish himself as one of the founding fathers of independent India? Ambedkar came from a financially stable family, which enabled him to have a primary school education. However, this access never could remove the 'untouchable' tag from his consciousness. The thought of being 'untouchable' plagued his mind, especially when he was denied the services of a barber or a driver because of it.

During his primary-school days, he was treated differently and ridiculed solely because he was a Mahar. This left a huge impact on him. However, Babasaheb took the fight to the orthodoxy, and at no point did he give up. For it is these very incidents that made him realize that the fight for the dignity of Dalits had to begin and be a constant one, until his very last breath. He recorded the experiences of untouchability faced by him in the newspaper *Janata*, which he founded in 1929.[5] Dhananjay Keer's biography, *Dr Babasaheb Ambedkar: Life and Mission*, published in 1954, also recounted all of Babasaheb's experiences.[6]

While his journey to educate himself was excruciating, he was determined to venture into the unknown. His secondary education was funded by the Maharaja Sayajirao Gaekwad III, the erstwhile ruler of Baroda (now Vadodara), and he studied at the Elphinstone High School in Bombay. Ambedkar's quest to arm himself with education never ceased, be it when he was in Columbia University, the London School of Economics or Gray's Inn, where he excelled in academics. The years spent in Europe and America made him feel the stark difference in the treatment he received there and the treatment meted out to him in India.

In 1942, when he founded the All India Scheduled Castes Federation (AISCF), which he later dissolved to found the Republican Party of India, he also initiated scholarships for Dalit students to study abroad.[7]

Ambedkar was always a firm advocate of education. He believed that if this revolution for the marginalized was to be won, access to quality education was crucial. He was never violent in his methods. He knew that equipping oneself with education would ensure a battle of dignity for the Dalits that could be fought and won. It was only after education that he felt empowered, for he believed only power could defeat power. Ambedkar being elected to the Bombay Legislative Council in 1926 and him founding the Independent Labour Party in 1936 are testimony to how crucial political representation was for Dalits.[8]

This focus on education was inculcated in him by his teacher at Columbia University, Professor John Dewey. Ambedkar has often said that he owes his intellectual life to Dewey, who was an American philosopher and psychologist but, above all, a reformer of education. Dewey was also one of the central figures associated with functional psychology, philosophy and progressive education.[9]

Very few Indian leaders have been educated in America. Ambedkar studied with the best minds at Columbia University in the three years he spent there. When he enrolled, he took a number of courses, including railroad economics. He was keen to learn from the top-ranking professors at the university.

All his life, Ambedkar sought the complete eradication of caste, for only this, he believed, would lead to an honourable society.

As Bhalchandra Mungekar writes in his introduction to *The Essential Ambedkar*, 'Ambedkar's basic arguments were against institutionalization of caste-based isolation and discrimination prevalent in the Hindu mind.'[10]

Ambedkar's words in his famous undelivered speech, which he later published in *Annihilation of Caste*, is relevant even today, as it shows the glaring fault lines in Hinduism and the urgent need to reform. His clarity of thought is discernible in his choice of words in the speech.

> Making the individual a sharer or partner in the associated activity, so that he feels its success as his success, its failure as his failure, is the real thing that binds men and makes a society of them. The caste system prevents common activity; and by preventing common activity, it has prevented the Hindus from becoming a society with a unified life and a consciousness of its own being.[11]

Annihilation of Caste is also a must-read, because it calls for a struggle for social justice without advocating any violent or punitive measures. This was Ambedkar's uniqueness. He even urged Dalits to establish a separate religion based on the principles of the Upanishads.[12]

However, Ambedkar was against communism just as much as he was against Hinduism for its glaring fault lines. In his famous speech 'Buddha or Karl Marx?', Ambedkar unequivocally called communism a violent philosophy, for it resorted to annihilate individuals for the sake of its ideology.[13]

Ambedkar was equally unrelenting towards socialists. He is known to have asked,

> Is it enough for a socialist to say, 'I believe in perfect equality in the treatment of the various classes?' To say that such a belief is enough is to disclose a complete lack of understanding of what

is involved in socialism. If socialism is a practical programme
and is not merely an ideal, distant and far off, the question for a
socialist is not whether he believes in equality. The question for
him is whether he minds one class ill-treating and suppressing
another class as a matter of system, as a matter of principle and
thus allows tyranny and oppression to continue to divide one
class from another.[14]

In essence, Ambedkar always believed that the critical test for any
philosophy of religion was 'revolution', that the number of times
a philosophy of religion had undergone revolution was the best
way to assess it. He consistently urged people to adopt this as the
method vis-à-vis their respective philosophy of religion in keeping
with the changing times.[15] Ambedkar also stressed that casteism
had crept into Christianity and Islam.[16]

Ambedkar was a voracious reader; he urged everyone to invest
10 per cent of one's income to buying books.[17] He himself had
more than 35,000 books as part of his personal library.[18] He was
not just widely read but well informed about a number of critical
issues as well. Some of these have helped shape modern India.
A bird's-eye view of his writings, speeches and works explain
that he was a multidimensional man. Be it in linguistics, foreign
policy, parliamentary democracy, economic development,
communism, the tenets of Buddhism or the politics of China,
Ambedkar put forth some sophisticated arguments in the
Constituent Assembly debates that went into the creation of
the Constitution as well as during his other speeches. He was
always ready for a solution when it came to issues concerning his
country. His unquestionable popularity amongst the depressed
classes added a much-needed democratic boost to his quest of
building a fair, equitable and inclusive document that would
guide the destiny of the whole of India.

Ambedkar had immense admiration for the Buddha and his
teachings. He believed that Buddhism was not just some practice

to be followed in privacy but was a powerful social force based on science that could offer solutions to the world.[19] He often spoke about how Buddha's mission was to change the mind of the man.[20] In one instance, he was merciless in his indictment of the US and called it a Christian country, underlining the need for it to be made accountable for its actions for bombing an Asian country, that too, a Buddhist one, in the backdrop of the Hiroshima and Nagasaki bombings.[21] One of the most striking aspects of his personality was that he believed in excellence through devotion. In his eyes, devotion was meant to be the 'extreme power of enduring suffering' and the 'extreme power of working'.[22]

He was an original thinker, never influenced by anyone or their views. His grasp of issues from a global context was another remarkable asset. A small case in point is his unique definition of democracy. Ambedkar defined democracy as 'a form of method of government whereby revolutionary changes in the economic and social life of the people are brought about without bloodshed'.[23]

Ambedkar had a deep sense of understanding of India's socio-economic and political problems. This equipped him to draft the Constitution and make effective, robust and scholarly interventions at the Constituent Assembly as well. He maintained that laws were to be made only by representatives of the people in Parliament. However, according to him, these laws had to be made based on the advice of the people who elected them. True to this, Ambedkar opined that if one had to preserve the institution of parliamentary democracy, then the people, especially the Dalits, had to be educated.[24] While educating the people was important, Ambedkar was against hereditary rule and was categorical in stating that the mandate of the people was essential for those seeking to govern and rule.[25]

Ambedkar also highlighted that any social boycott, especially any menace to the rights and liberties of people, had to be made punishable by law.[26] He was always looking for ways and means to give Dalits representation. In view of this, Ambedkar also tried to ensure that the central and state public service commissions allowed for adequate representation of all communities, including Dalits.[27]

Ambedkar encouraged the temple-entry movements, which began in 1924. He called them *satyagrahas*, but those that went unnoticed. This unique satyagraha movement went on for almost six years. At the end of it, untouchables were allowed entry into the Kalaram temple in Nashik, in the Bombay Presidency.[28]

In our minds, the strongest proponent of a united India was none other than Ambedkar. He maintained that the intellectual freedom found in ancient India could be found nowhere else.[29] There are two instances to illustrate this point.

First, when the Partition debates were at their peak, Ambedkar reinforced that no matter what the demands of the Muslim League were, Muslims themselves would think that a united India would be better.[30] This he elucidated by stating how the Constitution was a dual polity with a single citizenship. He said, 'There is only one citizenship for the whole of India. It is Indian citizenship. Every Indian has the same rights of citizenship, no matter in what state he resides.'[31] One of the things that he wanted to accomplish during his life, but unfortunately couldn't, was to write a history of the Indian Army.[32] Ambedkar was a patriot, but more than that, a pragmatic nation builder.

He kept a vigilant eye out for potential teething troubles during India's post-Independence phase in 1947. He even warned then prime minister Jawaharlal Nehru of the consequences of drifting towards China. He said,

The Prime Minister has been depending upon what may be called the 'Panchsheel',[33] taken by Mr. Mao and recorded in the Tibet treaty of non-aggression. Well I am somewhat surprised, that the Prime Minister should take this Panchsheel seriously. The Panchsheel, as you, Sir, know it well, is the essential part of Buddhist religion, if Mr. Mao had any faith in the Panchsheel, he would certainly treat the Buddhists in his country in a very different way. There is no room for Panchsheel in politics, and secondly, not in the politics of a communist country. The communists' countries have no morality. Today's morality is not tomorrow's morality.[34]

Very few people know this, but Ambedkar was also a violin player.[35]

Be it highlighting that social boycott should be made an offence punishable under law, or insisting adequate representation for Dalits in state and central public service commissions, or exposing the fault lines in Hinduism, communism and China, Ambedkar was the first in his time to air such viewpoints.

He was a leader whose popularity only grew with time. In a poll conducted jointly by the *Outlook* magazine, CNN-IBN and The History Channel in 2012, Ambedkar was voted the 'greatest Indian', outshining leaders such as Gandhi, Nehru and Patel.[36] Today, Ambedkar is a person who people across social groups (especially the youth) not just respect but love. Ambedkar died on 6 December 1956. But his social impact has only grown, and so has the adulation people feel for him.

If we are to focus on the relevance of Ambedkar, enabling citizens to be more aware and well informed about the Constitution is the need of the hour. If not, we the people, as the ultimate guardians of the Constitution, are doing a great disservice to his vision.

In today's time and age, the ideal homage to this towering soul is ensuring that the Dalits' social salvation is fast-tracked by annihilating caste, that we feel for the plight of the suppressed and ensure that their lives are as honourable as everyone else's and keep social reform at the forefront of our policies, before any economic or political reform. For this is what Ambedkar truly wanted—that social reform be at the heart of whatever we do to achieve in real and pragmatic terms, 'liberty, equality and fraternity'.

The NDA government, on the occasion of his 125th birth anniversary, in 2016, fittingly announced a set of legislative measures for Dalits to be relevant stakeholders in the growth story of India. With schemes such as Stand Up India, Pradhan Mantri Mudra Yojana and the National Scheduled Caste and Scheduled Tribe Hub for entrepreneurs, Dalits will be able to strongly register their presence in sectors that have traditionally been inaccessible to them. This is a befitting tribute to the tireless champion of the cause, Bharat Ratna B.R. Ambedkar, indeed a founding father of the nation.

Notes

1. Salim Yusufji, *Ambedkar: The Attendant Details*, Navayana Publishers, 2017.
2. Yusufji, *Ambedkar*, Foreword by Urmila Pawar, pp. 9–11.
3. Sachin Nagar's illustrations in Kieron Moore, *Ambedkar: India's Crusader for Human Rights*, Kalyani Navyug Media Pvt. Ltd, 2018.
4. Bhalchandra Mungekar, ed., *The Essential Ambedkar*, Rupa Publications India, 2016, p. 110.
5. Yusufji, *Ambedkar*, p. 155.
6. Ibid., p. 156.
7. Id., p. 188.
8. Id., p. 188.
9. Scott R. Stroud, 'The like-mindedness of Dewey and Ambedkar', Forward Press, 19 May 2017, https://www.forwardpress.in/2017/05/john-dewey-pragmatism-communication-and-bhimrao-ambedkar/
10. Mungekar. ed., *The Essential Ambedkar*.
11. Ambedkar, *Annhilation of Caste*, p. 244
12. Mungekar. ed., *The Essential Ambedkar*, p. 80.
13. Ibid., p. 350.
14. Id., p. 60.
15. Id., p. 71.
16. Id., p. 168.
17. Yusufji, *Ambedkar*, p. 95.
18. Ibid., p. 135.

19. Id., p. 10.
20. Mungekar. ed., *The Essential Ambedkar*, p. 356.
21. Yusufji, *Ambedkar*, p. 81.
22. Ibid., p. 143.
23. Mungekar. ed., *The Essential Ambedkar*, p. 289.
24. Sanjay Paswan and Paramanshi Jaideva, *Encyclopedia of Dalits in India*, Kalpaz Publications, p. 592004.
25. Mungekar. ed., *The Essential Ambedkar*, p. 303.
26. Ibid., p. 128.
27. Id., p. 132.
28. Id., pp. 153–54.
29. Id.
30. Id., p. 257.
31. Id., p. 264.
32. Yusufji, *Ambedkar*, p. 153.
33. Signed in 1954 under Jawaharlal Nehru, Panchsheel was an agreement of a set of principles signed between India and China to govern relations between the two countries.
34. Mungekar. ed., *The Essential Ambedkar*, p. 432.
35. Yusufji, *Ambedkar*, p. 152.
36. Uttam Sengupta, 'A Measure of the Man', *Outlook*, 20 August 2012, https://www.outlookindia.com/magazine/story/a-measure-of-the-man/281949.

Conclusion

Dalit Assertion to Seek Representation

The Hollywood film *Pay It Forward* has the powerful message of premise with promise. In the film, a seventh-grade teacher challenges his students to change the world. One student does so by creating an altruistic domino effect called Pay It Forward. The rules are simple: 1) It has to be something big that really helps people. 2) It must be something they can't do for themselves. 3) The benefactor has to aid three other people in need.

This inspiring movie comes to mind in view of today's Dalit icons. Not only have they really borne the brunt of society's intolerance towards lower castes, but they have also suffered other ills such as poverty, unemployment, child marriage, lack of education and more. Yet they have turned the stones thrown at them into milestones. These warriors are there amidst us all. They are silently striving to be something big that really helps people, and not just of their own community but of the entire nation.

In March 2018, India witnessed massive protests by Dalit organizations over the dilution of the Scheduled Castes and

Scheduled Tribes (Prevention of Atrocities) Act. The protests were a response to the Supreme Court's directive barring automatic arrests and the provision of anticipatory bail for the accused in cases of atrocities against Dalits and tribal communities. It also ruled that public servants would not be prosecuted without the approval of the appointing authority. The Supreme Court overturned the verdict, acknowledging the unimaginable levels of oppression faced by the socially disadvantaged sections of society.[1] Their protests were another powerful symbol of Dalit assertion. But in this concluding chapter we have tried to showcase the assertion of Dalits in various fields of work where they have reached the top despite starting from the very bottom of the social ladder.

Each of them has taken inspiration from one or many of the heroes that have been mentioned in the book. They have been genuinely impacted by these heroes and hence continue to live their values every day. If one has to carefully observe the manner in which they have gone about their careers, it becomes apparent that they have not opted for the conventional method of protests or confrontation, nor have they sought refuge in it. They have set out on a journey to engage with society with cooperation and empowerment through the medium of capital, artificial intelligence, information technology, education and jobs, to name a few.

The cohesive minds of these achievers are armed with what generation-next needs today. While they are anchored in some of the pristine ideals of the past, they are keen to set forth on a debate on the needs of the present. It is natural to agonize over the bruises they have been dealt in the past. Yet, these icons, who we will discuss in this chapter, do not let that deter them. Instead, they constantly look for ways and means to be seen, heard and understood on merit, effort, values, hard work and energy.

Every movement, innovation and change happens only when we challenge the status quo with new, out-of-the-box ideas. By pursuing their passion, each of today's Dalit heroes has brought new ideas to the fore, and in times when status quo is often leant back on, they have set new standards by challenging it.

What is also striking is that these heroes of today do not shy away from discussing the bane of caste in everyday conversations. In fact, through the medium of their respective achievements, they showcase to the world how caste can be defeated and are determined to emancipate their fellow community members.

They have committed themselves to the larger cause of nation-building. But even after receiving laurels for the achievements, they do not sit back and relax. They believe in work and helping everyone achieve their dreams. If you want to change the system, enter it, study it and then change it from within. These present-day icons—in various fields and not just politics—symbolize a fearless focus to bring about change.

Milind Kamble

Milind Kamble is a name that resonates with not just the prime minister of India today but with millions of Dalit entrepreneurs too. Hailing from Maharashtra, Kamble evolved into a visionary, launching the Dalit Indian Chamber of Commerce and Industry (DICCI). His success in the unabashed use of capitalism to empower the scheduled communities continues to inspire many. Kamble lives by the simple motto, 'Dalits should pursue to defeat caste with capital.'[2] His vision of founding DICCI is premised on the principle that Dalits must 'evolve as job providers and not seekers'.

Through DICCI, Kamble has been relentlessly helping people from the SC and ST communities to bid for projects under the Sagar Mala (the initiative of setting up and modernizing mega ports), highways and road construction, and projects floated by the petroleum ministry under the Government of India.

DICCI is helping people sharpen their innovative ideas so they can be pitched to the Department of Industrial Policy

& Promotion (DIPP) for incubation centres. True to Kamble's motto, he is steering several schemes of the government, such as Stand-Up India and the setting up of the National Schedule Caste Schedule Tribe Hub under the Ministry of Micro, Small and Medium Enterprises, among others. Within a decade of setting up DICCI, Kamble has encouraged more than 3,000 entrepreneurs.

Tina Dabi

The story of Tina Dabi is one of deep and complex social change in India, which has made her the first Dalit girl to top the UPSC examination. As former Lok Sabha MP and ex-civil servant Udit Raj tweeted, 'This would not have been possible 40-50 years ago.'[3]

On her achievement, former civil servant P.S. Krishnan said,

> It makes clear what removing obstacles and taking away roadblocks and difficulties can do. Cases like these inspire a lot as they are a testament to how meritorious deprived communities can be, and their innate talent shines and cuts through all issues. This is a sign of great success and possibility for Dalits struggling to break free of their circumstances.[4]

Dabi says she owes her success to her parents instilling in her the belief that education was a key catalyst for emancipation. In an interview to the *Indian Express*, Dabi's father, Jaswant, indeed credited his own father's struggles and efforts when it came to the achievements of Tina and the family. 'The real struggle was waged by my father and grandfather who was [*sic*] in the military and left it soon. My father taught in order to be able to study and make money to fund my education. We have never forgotten all that,' he said.[5]

As is evident from Dabi's interviews, she feels strongly about gender issues and wants to work on this in any district or state, which has a skewed gender ratio. She says,

I think Rajasthan has its own women related issues. If we talk about the child sex ratio in Rajasthan, it's not as much as we'd like it to be. But we have a very strong system of women holding key positions in the panchayats over there. It's a very promising thing and it's something that even I would want to encourage in whichever district I'm posted in. I also want to make sure state government and union government's schemes are implemented properly and monitor the targets.[6]

Dabi is also a firm believer in being an integral part of the system one wants to change—this is key to bringing about any change, she believes. In an address to students in Delhi's Lady Sri Ram College, Dabi said,

If you really think that you can bring about a change in the system, then get into the system and make that change. It is a man's world and to fight back we have to develop a very thick skin. Take criticism very constructively, but at the same time fight back and retain your position.[7]

Arjun Ram Meghwal

Arjun Ram Meghwal, who is currently serving as the union minister of state for Ministry of Water Resources, River Development & Ganga Rejuvenation and Parliamentary Affairs in Government of India, is another visionary Dalit. 'I have the impact of Ambedkar, I have read Ambedkar and I live Ambedkar,' he roared at a seminar in Chennai in 2017 on the importance of social integration.[8]

From being a weaver, to working his way up to the Indian Administrative Service (IAS) as an officer, to being elected as MP, to becoming a union minister, Meghwal's journey has been an inspiration to many. Meghwal was born into a traditional weaver family in Kismidesar village, Bikaner, and was married at the young age of thirteen.[9] He, however, continued to work with his father as a weaver while pursuing his career goals. He graduated with a BA degree from Sri Dungar College in Bikaner and also earned himself an LLB and a master's degree from the same institution. After his studies, he started preparing for competitive examinations and got into the union telephone department in Ganganagar district in Rajasthan as a telephone operator. Meghwal had his first stint with politics when he contested and won the elections for the post of general secretary of the Telephone Traffic Association. A three-time MP from Rajasthan, Meghwal was one of the few MPs to cycle up to Rashtrapathi Bhavan for his swearing-in ceremony as minister of state.[10]

Narendra Jadhav

Another son of the soil who has worked tirelessly for the cause of Dalits is Narendra Jadhav. While there are many generalists, the country is indeed grateful and blessed to have a specialist on Babasaheb Ambedkar—and that is Jadhav. An MP from Rajya Sabha and an economist, Jadhav has also successfully penned the memoirs of his family, *Untouchables*, a compelling story that has been published in many languages, from Marathi to Spanish, Korean, Thai, French and many other Indian languages, and which has run into many editions. He often articulates his vision through Ambedkar's words even today. 'For me, India always comes first. I am an Indian first and last. My passion in life is inclusive growth and development across all sections of the Indian society and all regions of my country,' he said.[11]

Holding a doctorate in economics from Indiana University in the US, Jadhav has earlier served in several distinguished positions, including as member of the Planning Commission, member of the National Advisory Council, vice chancellor of the Savitribhai Phule Pune University, and chief economist of the Reserve Bank of India. He has written or edited thirty-seven books, including twelve on Ambedkar—six each in English and Marathi—comprising an intellectual biography, speeches (three volumes each) and Ambedkar's writings (two volumes each). Jadhav is also the recipient of as many as sixty-seven national and international awards for his contribution to the fields of economics, education, literature, culture and social work. These include four honorary DLitt degrees and the title of the commander of the Order of Academic Palms by the government of France. He is a true ambassador of Ambedkar's vision.[12]

Kalpana Saroj

Another inspiring entrepreneur who has defied all odds to climb up the social ladder and helm a $112-million empire is Kalpana Saroj. Here is an icon who has overcome poverty, child marriage and inhuman abuse. Determination, grit, perseverance and faith in self have helped Saroj become the woman she is today. Born in Vidarbha, she was subject to severe discrimination. Be it at her residential quarters or at the school she studied in, people's behaviour towards her because she was a Dalit shocked and often hurt her. They even went to the extent of telling their children not to engage with her, be it during their playtime or even when it came to sharing their food at lunchtime.

Although her father wanted her to complete her education, Saroj was pulled out of school and married off at the age of twelve. She was responsible for cooking, cleaning, laundry and other chores of a household of about ten people. Her family could not afford two square meals a day, and in this situation her younger sister fell ill. To treat her they needed Rs 2000, which they couldn't afford. The death of her sibling made Saroj realize that she had to work hard and achieve what she wanted, as she saw how scarce money was.

From then on, she started working sixteen hours a day, a habit she still maintains. She said in one of her interviews, 'Hard work is not overrated. It is fail proof. What you want—whatever it is—you shall get, if you apply yourself wholeheartedly and work towards it with a single minded vision.'[13] When Kamani Tubes Limited approached her for help, the company had been closed for more than seventeen years and was registered as a sick industrial unit. Braving heavy litigation, Saroj took on the role of chairperson and got it back on its feet. The rest, as they say, is history.[14]

Meira Kumar

Another inspiring story of women-led empowerment is of Meira Kumar. Born in Bihar's Arrah district, she is the daughter of prominent Dalit leader and former deputy prime minister Jagjivan Ram and Indrani Devi, who was a freedom fighter. Kumar is a law graduate and holds a master's degree in English literature. In 1973, she qualified for the Indian Foreign Service and served at embassies in Mauritius, Spain and the United Kingdom. After quitting from Foreign Service in 1985, she decided to pursue a career in politics. In her first contest from Uttar Pradesh's Bijnor, she defeated political heavyweights such as Ram Vilas Paswan and Mayawati.

In 2004, Kumar was appointed the minister of social justice and empowerment under then Prime Minister Manmohan Singh in the Congress-led United Progressive Alliance (UPA) government. In 2009, she was inducted into the Cabinet as union minister of water resources. Soon after, from 2009 to 2014, Kumar served as the country's first female Dalit speaker of the Lok Sabha.

Political observers have written that this Opposition candidate might have lost the presidential poll to Ram Nath Kovind, who was fielded by the BJP and its NDA allies, but in securing nearly 34.35 per cent of the valid votes, she had put up a tough fight. In fact, her performance was the best by any losing candidate since the 1969 election, when even though V.V. Giri defeated Neelam Sanjiva Reddy, the latter polled nearly 37.5 per cent votes.

Bhalchandra Mungekar

Another present-day hero who has fought all odds, especially poverty and caste discrimination, is Bhalchandra Mungekar. In fact, when the Manmohan Singh government reconstituted the Planning Commission and nominated new members, one name that caught the attention of the media was his. He was given the charge of education, labour and employment, social justice and tribal affairs.

Mungekar's remarkable journey to the corridors of the Parliament began from a small village called Munge in the Konkan region of Maharashtra. A former Rajya Sabha MP, Mungekar was born into a poor Dalit family. The reason for nominating Mungekar to the erstwhile Planning Commission and Rajya Sabha was his outstanding achievements in the field of academia. He is an economist of repute specializing in agricultural economics; he was, and still is, involved in various social activities; and he is an expert on B.R. Ambedkar. He was also the vice chancellor of Mumbai University, a post he vacated to join the Planning Commission. One aspect of his life, however, remains unchanged—how he ensures that help reaches the poor. Perhaps this is why he remains an inspiration to gen-next.

Sukhdeo Thorat

Who can forget Sukhdeo Thorat, who, with his writings and social activities, has worked tirelessly towards the empowerment of the Dalits, tribals and Denotified Tribes. The World Bank has acknowledged his achievements with the following words:

> Prof. Thorat was involved in the civil rights movement against untouchability and caste discrimination and struggled to get entry into his village temple in the early 1960s. He supported MPs, particularly from Dalits, in their work in the Parliament

and also SC/ST Parliamentary Forum on several issues. He also founded the Indian Institute of Dalit Studies. As Chairman of the University Grants Commission, he assisted the government in higher education, particularly the UPA and Prime Minister Dr. Manmohan Singh, in their initiatives to take higher education ahead.[15]

Apart from supporting and working for reservation for Dalits, Thorat has also consistently advocated for the right to property and education, turning it into a brilliant example of Dalit-led empowerment.

Radhika Gill

A track and field athlete from Jammu and Kashmir, Radhika Gill, in her indomitable manner, has fought for the rights of the Valmiki community in the state. Her community, the Valmiki Dalits, were made to migrate from Punjab to Jammu and Kashmir in 1957 by the then government, to be employed as sweepers and scavengers.[16] As compensation, the Valmikis were assured that the permanent resident clause of the state would be relaxed for them. However, the reality was far from the promises made by the government. According to Gill, the 200 odd Valmiki families, even till date, have not been able to obtain a community certificate, let alone a permanent residency in the state.[17] This led Gill to challenge the constitutional validity of Article 35A. Gill was refused a civil services job and even told that she could only be a sweeper.[18] She was considered an outsider in her own state and was consistently asked for a domicile certificate to prove her identity and seek employment.

Hailing from a marginalized community, her battle to fight for the right to dignity, not just for her self but for her community brethren, makes Gill an invaluable unsung icon.

Rangaswamy Elango

A scientist born in a Dalit family, Rangaswamy Elango worked at the Council of Scientific and Industrial Research and has turned seven hamlets in Tamil Nadu into an epitome of equality. Apart from inequality, his village and neighbouring hamlets, which had about 50 per cent Dalit population, were fighting battles on many fronts. Illicit liquor trade, drunken brawls, miserable health conditions and broken family relationships were leading to nothing but poverty in the areas. In 2000, under the leadership of Elango, for the first time in India, fifty twin houses were built in a single colony called 'Samathuvapuram' (place for equality), where, in every twin house, one Dalit and one non-Dalit family coexisted in harmony. The scheme was later adopted by the Tamil Nadu government and extended to the entire state.

Elango, a former panchayat president himself, took to the task of training over 1000 panchayat presidents in Tamil Nadu to ensure equality in the areas.[19]

Ram Vilas Paswan

The states of Uttar Pradesh and Bihar have produced some of the finest leaders in recent times. A couple of names that stand out are former union minister Ram Vilas Paswan from Bihar, Sanjay Paswan, member of the Bihar Legislative Council, and the current president of India, Ram Nath Kovind, from Uttar Pradesh.

Ram Vilas Paswan had a remarkable innings as a political activist and an able administrator. He was a part of several ministries since 1989, such as railways, communications, chemicals and fertilizers and mines, in various governments under the UPA, NDA and the United Front. Until his death in October 2020, he was the union minister of consumer affairs, food and public distribution. Paswan's entry to the Lok Sabha on a Janata

Party ticket was from Hajipur in Bihar, with a record margin of 4,25,545 votes in the 1977 general elections. This catapulted him to the Guinness World Records, which was later broken by P.V. Narasimha Rao, the then prime minister.

Sanjay Paswan

Sanjay Paswan, who was a union minister in the late prime minister Atal Bihari Vajpayee's government, is a leading public intellectual and political leader in the country today. Currently serving as member of the Bihar Legislative Council, he is a spiritualist at heart, continues to teach in Patna University and is always available for a dialogue on cohesion and equality at the university and various other public and political platforms.

Through his initiative, Kabir Ke Log, Paswan continues to anchor important intellectual dialogues to articulate the new Dalit agenda in the twenty-first century. By marking important occasions related to their lives, he continues to bring forth forgotten Dalit heroes, such as Bhola Paswan Shastri, who was Bihar's chief minister for three terms.

Ram Nath Kovind

'A Dalit was elected India's 14th president, a rare achievement for a member of a community once known as "untouchables" and one of the most deprived groups in India,' reported the *New York Times* when Ram Nath Kovind was elected India's president.[20] He holds the honour of being India's second Dalit president after late K.R. Narayanan.

In November 2001, when Kovind visited Paraukh, his ancestral village in Kanpur Dehat district of Uttar Pradesh, the Thakurs and Brahmins decided to honour him by presenting twelve precious *mukut*s (ceremonial crowns), eleven made of silver and one of gold. Then a Rajya Sabha member of the BJP, Kovind, however, politely declined accepting the mukuts. This did not come as a surprise to those who knew him. 'It was typical of him. He has always been very simple and selfless. He asked us to save the money and mukuts to fund the marriage of poor girls of the village,' recalled Jaswant Singh, Kovind's childhood friend.[21]

In 2017, as soon as the BJP announced his name for the presidential elections—which saw 5,000 lawmakers of India in action as part of the electoral college, which consists of elected members of both Houses of Parliament and the elected members of the legislative assemblies of all the states, the NCT of Delhi and the Union Territory of Puducherry—many actually looked him up online to get a glimpse of who he was.

Kovind, serving in office since 25 July 2017, is the fourteenth president of India. He has previously served as the governor of Bihar from 2015 to 2017 and as an MP, Rajya Sabha, from 1994 to 2006. Before entering politics, he was a lawyer for sixteen years, practising in the Delhi High Court and the Supreme Court until 1993.

After winning the presidential election, Kovind said in his speech, 'Today there are many Ram Nath Kovinds who are getting wet in the rain, working hard in the fields for one square meal. I'll represent all those struggling to make a living.'[22]

The emergence of Ma Venkatesan in Tamil Nadu, Jignesh Mevani in Gujarat and Chandrashekar Azad in western Uttar Pradesh represent one component of Dalit assertion in India today, while the stories of Milind Kamble, Tina Dabi and Rangaswamy Elango represent the other aspirational component of the contemporary Dalit struggle.

There are also several writers, such as Gopal Guru and K. Satyanarayana, from the community, who have made a name for themselves on the world stage.[23]

Civil society, industry, the media, higher judiciary and the upper echelons of bureaucracy still lack social diversity and, therefore, the empathy required to address the concerns of the community.

Having said that, what we can certainly expect more of is our Dalit brethren in leadership roles in the IITs and IIMs. The Ministry of Human Resource Development, in a recent notification, asked the IITs, IIMs and other premier institutions of the country to follow reservation norms in faculty recruitment. Unfortunately, people from marginalized communities did not have any leadership role in these institutions for a long time. However, we hope that many more heroes will emerge in the days to come, bringing about a radical change in the state of affairs in the country.[24]

Here, we have attempted to highlight the achievements of some present-day Dalit heroes who have made it to the pinnacle of their careers. This, by no means, is to say that their achievements end here—they have a lot more to offer the nation and its people. What is most inspiring is that there are innumerable Kovinds, Gills, Elangos, Mungekars, Kambles, Sarojs, Kumars, Paswans, Thorats and Meghwals in India; we hope this book is an inspiration to all of them in their life pursuits and an encouragement for all to defy the evil of caste. We hope it will guide them to creating their unique identities, as others from their communities have done before them.

Protect, Preserve and Promote Our Dalit Heroes

French anthropologist Nicolas Jaoul in his academic paper, 'Learning the Use of Symbolic Means: Dalits, Ambedkar Statues and the State in Uttar Pradesh', published in 2006, writes, 'In the context of poverty and illiteracy where they operate, such symbolic means have profound political implications, promoting ideals of citizenship and nationhood among the politically destitute where the state has partially failed.' If such is the impact of museums and memorials of our Dalit heroes, then imagine the impact of words written about them.[25]

Even as India builds memorials and museums to preserve the country's sociopolitical movements, including the Dalit community's achievements, we believe what needs more attention is scholarships on the life and work of present-day icons from the subaltern communities. This, in turn, will encourage and support the efforts of the future generations to know more about them. What also needs our due attention is the preservation and documentation of the achievements of these modern-day Dalit heroes. We believe that literature on the subject can prove to be a great source of inspiration and empowerment for disadvantaged communities. In addition, this can also act as a catalyst of self-assertion for Dalits today.

This book is just a small addition in the ever-expanding oeuvre of Dalit literature globally. It is a conversation of sorts, and a small repayment of the huge debt that we as a society owe to the tenacious Dalit community and its leadership. As late P.S. Krishnan once remarked, 'Indian society owes the Scheduled Castes a heavy moral and material debt.'[26]

Vivek Kumar, a professor at the Centre for the Study of Social Systems, School of Social Sciences, at the Jawaharlal Nehru University, who is also an inspirational figure for the Dalit community, puts it succinctly, reiterating that writing about Dalits is the need of the hour:

> These are the people who were devoid of cultural capital for thousands of years, whose struggles were never even recognized, whose stories and rightful contribution did not make it to the history books their struggles need to be counted in the process of nation building.[27]

We hope this book inspires every Indian and helps them connect with the extraordinary stories of these icons. These are the kind of stories that we, as a nation, will cherish not only reading but documenting, the kind of remarkable stories that we will continue to share with the world for a very simple reason—the world needs more of them.

Life Lessons

To conclude, all the individuals we have written about have, in one way or the other, imparted life lessons to us. These are:

1. **Have a vision:** All of them had a vision to fight and challenge the status quo and banish the evil of of caste and untouchability from society. They fought not with punitive measures but with education, devotion, poetry and writing.

2. **Battle difficult circumstances with bravery:** In fighting the circumstances around them, the bravery displayed by each of them is astounding. Despite having to face poverty, unemployment, lack of education and basic amenities and intense discrimination, they didn't give up. It is their tremendous bravery in the face of social adversities that stands out in their lives.

3. **Work hard towards victory:** In seeking representation and a cohesive society, all these heroes have worked tirelessly to become more aware and work themselves up the social ladder. We must always remember to work hard to gain victory in whatever we do.

4. **Efforts must continue and should not go in vain:** It is our responsibility to ensure that the efforts of these Dalit achievers in pursuit of an equal and cohesive society do not go in vain.

5. **Do not look at our Dalit brethren as mere votes:** We must ensure that we move beyond tokenism, such as dining with them or visiting their homes. Instead of looking at them as vote banks, we should look at them as thought banks contributing to the bright future of our country.

Anil Gupta, in his book *Grassroots Innovation*, has stated, 'Minds on the margin are not marginal minds.' This is a constructive approach to enabling Dalit assertion and representation in a just way.

Notes

1. Sanjay Paswan, 'A constructive approach, not polemic, is needed to address Dalit concerns', *Indian Express*, 11 October 2019, https://indianexpress.com/article/opinion/columns/sc-st-prevention-of-atrocities-act-supreme-court-national-crime-records-bureau-6063190/.

2. Shubhangi Khapre, 'Dalits and tribals should defeat caste with capital, says Milind Kamble, DICCI chief', *Indian Express*, 8 February 2016, https://indianexpress.com/article/cities/mumbai/dalits-and-tribals-should-defeat-caste-with-capital-says-milind-kamble-dicci-chief/.

3. Sakshi Dayal, 'UPSC results: 22-year-old topper Tina Dabi picks "big paradox"' Haryana as cadre', *Financial Express*, 11 May 11 2016, https://www.financialexpress.com/jobs/upsc-results-22-year-old-topper-tina-dabi-picks-big-paradox-haryana-as-cadre/252632/.

4. Seema Chisti, 'Between the lines of Tina Dabi's IAS success story: Individual excellence and social change', *Indian Express*, 1 July 2016, https://indianexpress.com/article/india/india-news-india/tina-dabi-upsc-topper-upsc-civil-services-examination-2797804/.

5. Chisti, 'Between the lines of Tina Dabi's IAS success story: Individual excellence and social change'.

6. Aranya Sankar, 'UPSC topper Tina Dabi at LSR: "Would like to work on women-related issues"', *Indian Express*, 28 July 2016, https://indianexpress.com/article/education/upsc-topper-tina-dabi-lsr-speech-2941078/.

7. 'It's a man's world, but fight back: UPSC topper Tina Dabi tells LSR students', *Hindustan Times*, 29 July 2016, https://www.hindustantimes.com/india-news/it-s-a-man-s-world-but-fight-back-upsc-topper-tina-dabi-tells-students/story-L4OLccQbYi5tdbM8GNMECO.html; Riya Sharma, Tina Dabi: If you want to change the system, get into it and change it: https://timesofindia.indiatimes.com/city/delhi/tina-dabi-if-you-want-to-change-the-system-get-into-it-and-change-it/articleshow/57575983.cms.

8. https://www.youtube.com/watch?v=8wd7gEP1uwM&feature=youtu.be.

9. Indo-Asian News Service, 'From Weaver to IAS to Minister, Arjun Ram Meghwal Is Inspiration for Many', NDTV, 5 July 2016, https://www.ndtv.com/people/from-weaver-to-ias-to-minister-arjun-ram-meghwal-is-inspiration-for-many-1428175.

10. Ibid.

11. 'Vision and Mission', http://www.drnarendrajadhav.info/drjadhav-data_files/Career-Objective.htm.

12. 'Brief Biography', http://www.drnarendrajadhav.info/drjadhav-data_files/About-Dr-Narendra-Jadhav.htm.

13. Rakhi Chakraborty, 'Dalit Child Bride to $112 Million CEO: The Wonder Story of Kalpana Saroj', YourStory, 2015, https://yourstory.com/2015/02/kalpana-saroj/.

14. Ibid.

15. 'Prof. Sukhadeo Thorat', World Bank Live, 2013, http://live.worldbank.org/experts/prof-sukhadeo-thorat.

16. Ratan Sharda, 'Invisible Victims of Partition', *DNA*, 13 August 2019.

17. Ibid.

18. 'Heartbreaking story of Article 35A Victim Radhika Gill', YouTube, 30 November 2018, https://www.youtube.com/watch?v=uOr3EQFjdYw.

19. Think Change India, 'The story of a Dalit leader who quit his govt job to end his village's illegal alcohol trade', YourStory, 18 October 2017, https://yourstory.com/2017/10/rangaswamy-elango-dalit-kuthambakkam-village-chennai.

20. Nida Najar, 'India Picks Ram Nath Kovind, of Caste Once Called "Untouchables," as President', *New York Times*, 22 December 2017, https://www.nytimes.com/2017/07/20/world/asia/india-dalit-president-ram-nath-kovind.html.

21. Omar Rashid, 'Ram Nath Kovind, Paraukh and the Road to Raisina Hill', *The Hindu*, 20 June 2017, https://www.thehindu.com/news/national/ram-nath-kovind-paraukhs-celebrated-son/article19110041.ece.

22. 'President-elect Ram Nath Kovind's acceptance speech: Full text', Presented at New Delhi on 20 July 2017, *India Today*, https://www.indiatoday.in/india/story/president-elect-ram-nath-kovinds-acceptance-speech-full-text-1025459-2017-07-20

23. Joshil K. Abraham and Judith Misrahi-Barak, eds, *Dalit Literatures in India*, Routledge, 2018, p. 14.

24. Guru Prakash, 'Reservation needs fresh approach to align with times, empower marginalised', *Indian Express*, 17 December 2019, https://indianexpress.com/article/opinion/columns/fitting-tribute-to-ambedkar-reservation-dalits-6170484

25. Ashwaq Masoodi, 'Why memorials and statues are so important to Dalits', *Livemint*, 8 June 2017, https://www.livemint.com/Politics/uRX8YdI9IgpvUlCnnFh9jM/Why-memorials-and-statues-are-so-important-to-Dalits.html.

26. Guru Prakash, 'For P S Krishnan, welfare of Dalits, Adivasis, trumped ideological considerations', *Indian Express*, 15 November 2019, https://indianexpress.com/article/opinion/columns/an-officer-for-social-justice-6120243/.

27. Masoodi, 'Why memorials and statues are so important to Dalits'.

Acknowledgements

Every great endeavour stands on the pillars of a team— a team made up of inspired members who offer their inputs, advice and skill. Right from the outset, the team at Penguin Random House India, led and championed by Meru Gokhale, not only enabled us to structure our thought process but also handheld us in successfully completing the written matter of the book.

Ranjana Sengupta offered key inputs and timely guidance. Anushree Kaushal has been patient and encouraging at every stage.

We would also like to thank the copy-editor, Ujjaini Dasgupta, as well as the brilliant cover designer, Devangana Dash, and the untiring Marketing team for their relentless efforts. Cibani Premkumar was also part of the editorial process in the formative stages of the book.

Shantanu Ray Chaudhuri has enabled seamless supervision of the copy-editorial stage of the book. And how can we forget the sales, marketing, design, production, customer service and editorial teams who have been a part of *Makers of Modern Dalit History*! Thank you to each and every one of you.

We would fail in our duty if we miss Shiny Das and Premanka Goswami, who gave important inputs and saw the book through to publishing.

Much before we had ever imagined we could author a book, several people gave us that much-needed push off the edge of the cliff that really enabled us to start writing about the icons of the Dalit movement. That is indeed how the seeds were sown and there has been no turning back since. Our heartfelt gratitude to each and every one of them.

Several well-wishers have spared precious time in providing assistance with the research and contents of the book. They have been sounding boards every time we needed important and insightful inputs. We acknowledge their support with heartfelt gratitude.

Our families have been rock-solid in their support and in understanding why this was such an important project and phase for us. The words 'thank you' are inadequate for such consistent and silent love.

Team India Foundation, we are because you are.

Finally, our utmost gratitude to the Makers of Modern Dalit History themselves and to every single author and publisher that has ever focused on them. We know the value of their work and we relate to what they would have felt. With each and every word researched and written, the personalities have unfolded and had a personal impact on us. Each one is not just a subject but also a source of inspiration and life guidance; indeed, each one is a constant companion, and we hope that this book proves to be such a companion to you, the reader.